From Hustler to InvestHER

A Simple 6-Step Escape Plan for Business Women Who
Want Passive Income

Sarah Nicole Nadler, Destiny Bounds

Contents

Legal Disclaimer

T he contents of this book are not intended to be taken as any type of professional advice, legal, tax, financial or otherwise, but general information and education for the public. There is no special relationship between you and Sarah or you and Destiny by merely reading this book. Even though Destiny is an attorney, she is writing this book in her capacity as a representative for her consulting company, Bound for Destiny Consulting (completely separate from her legal services provided by Bounds Law LLC), and as purely legal education under her separate company, Bounds Enterprises LLC, where all information is for educational purposes only. While Destiny is a licensed attorney and certified small business consultant, the insights and information in this book should not be construed as personalized legal or professional advice. Readers should seek independent legal or professional consultation for specific advice tailored to their individual circumstances.

We hope you truly enjoy the information provided herein and invite you to reach out to either of us for more information on how we can talk about your specific situation and assist.

FREE GIFT

To say thanks for grabbing a copy of this book, Destiny & Sarah would like to gift you FREE access to the replay of our popular 5-Day Wealth MagnifyHER Challenge!
We know you are more likely to implement the strategies in this book if you watch the challenge training too.
Instead of paying $100 for the replay on our website, we'd like to give it to you for free...
bit.ly/fffbookbundle

Meet Sarah

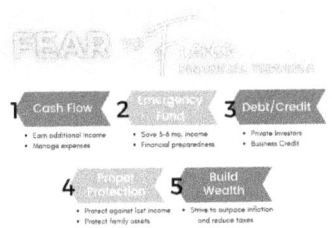

I used to be addicted to hustle culture.

Growing up, I was taught that hard work was the way to "get ahead", and because my first business was a residential cleaning company I built when I was 19, I've never been afraid of getting my hands dirty.

Oh, and I never invested a dime until I was 30.

Stepping off that beaten path and beginning my own journey to financial freedom has allowed me to create my dream lifestyle, get on track to retire before my 45th birthday, and earn tens of thousands in passive income every year since.

If you're reading this book because you are tired of the hustle culture predominant in the entrepreneur world, and hoping for a way to earn money without having to trade your time for it, you should know, I wrote this book for 2 reasons:

Reason #1: To give you a simple financial strategy you can use to build wealth by monetizing your magic, and thereby become financially free.

Reason #2: So you don't have to suffer the kind of agony I have seen women feel when they believe they "waited too late" to start investing and planning for retirement.

The strategy taught in this book is the safest way I've found for building wealth and becoming financially bulletproof. We call it *The Fear To Fierce Financial Formula.*

It is not based on guesswork or theory.

I went from ZERO savings, retirement plans or investments at age 30... to being on track to retire before my 45th birthday with more than half of my monthly bills already being paid by my investment portfolio with multiple streams of passive income.

Today I live on my dream spread; a 16-acre off-grid homestead outside Kansas City where I live the "barefoot lifestyle", grow my own food, host weddings and retreats, and enjoy slow living with my husband Ben.

I've had the privilege of teaching this formula to college graduating classes, in global magazine articles like *She Rises,* on stages, podcasts, and local television.

So, it's a great pleasure to finally have a chance to sit down and scribble it out for you. **I wanted to put an end to women struggling financially or putting their families at financial risk to invest, and that meant I had to educate women on the options for financial freedom that most of us never learn.**

That's why I decided to partner with Destiny and write this book.

Happy reading!

Meet Destiny

In the early 2010's, I was a first-year associate (lawyer) at a medium-sized law firm in Kansas City. I was working 70-80 hours a week and traveling every other week.

Hustle culture is prevalent in law firms, as it is everywhere else, and was a very real part of my everyday life...

One day I found myself sitting with my hands clasped tightly on my lap, waiting for my first review with the top partners of the firm. I sat across from them, trying to appear calm and collected, my feet gently crossed and swept to the left side of my chair. My suit was on point, flaunting a dark blue blazer, white and blue pinstripe blouse, and matching dark blue skirt with my gold jewelry. My heels -- pointed toes, the perfect two inches, and matching dark blue color. I must have looked like I just walked out of a Banana Republic ad.

But inside I was beginning to sweat. *This is awful*, I thought. You know that tight feeling when anxiety starts to settle in your chest? It was my first "real" mid-annual review as an associate. And, as expected, the partners were too focused on my "billable hours" and what my "realization" rate was (in other words, they didn't care how burned out I felt or how happy my clients were, just how much I was earning the firm).

I started to feel used. These top partners didn't care how good of a job I did, or whether I was happy. They cared about how much they could bill my clients, and how long they could get me to stay at the office.

And then it came.

The first real demeaning comment of my career. The one that made me realize I needed to forge my own path, and not one built on the daily grind or "billable hours". The moment that drove home the truth that I was meant for something more.

One of the partners sat straight across from me. He had been my enemy, a thorn in my side; my Achilles heel, if you will, since my first day. He typically had nothing nice to say. It just wasn't his style. It just wasn't in "his" culture–the "legal" culture–for a big partner at a firm to say anything nice to anybody new in the firm, so I didn't expect any compliments, but apparently he was ready to take it to a whole new level this time.

He spoke up in my review saying–

"Ya know, your billing [amount of hours I was working] *looks great. You're on track for hitting 2000 hours. That's great at this point. Ya know, you really are just doing well for a first-year female associate."*

And, there it was. All I could think was, "Dude, *really?!?* What does being female have anything to do with my performance?!?"

Everything apparently. The real crappy thing is that I believe he even meant it as a compliment in his backward way.

The only thing I could muster was a small laugh and a rise of an eyebrow. Clearly, my facial expression (because heaven only knows I can't hide my emotions) caused suspicion of the other partners.

The managing partner cleared his throat and spoke up, *"Well now he doesn't mean 'female,' haha."*

Sure he didn't, sure.

The third partner, well let's just say when I looked over at him--he was staring at the ground, intently, and wide-eyed--real wide-eyed at the floor. I'm sure he was thinking: *"Oh lawdy, we're getting sued."*

The sexism of corporate America isn't the point here. That was just the icing on the cake.

Our self-worth should not be tied to how many hours we work. When a woman is glamorized by a firm because she can put in the "most" hours of billable time, or because she stayed at the office the longest, we have lost sight of something vital in how we measure the wealth of a human being.

We live in a culture where our self-worth is commonly equated to how "busy" we are or how many appointments we can fill our calendar with. But putting in time is meaningless if it doesn't bring about exceptional results, or at least results that are satisfactory!

Our work also shouldn't result in back-handed compliments because we're *fierce females* in a world still unfortunately dominated by men, leaving us in the shadows.

As women, we know hard work is required. We're not afraid of it. But when all your hard work only earns you burnout, exhaustion and sexist quips from the men above you...what's a gal to do?

Learn how to go from Hustler to InvestHER, that's what.

My dad was a serial entrepreneur. He dabbled in everything from selling mobile homes, flipping properties, to buying a large RV park and serving hundreds of tenants over the years. It was always about "bringing in money while you sleep," but he struggled a lot, mainly due to taking shortcuts that got him into legal trouble because he didn't have a business attorney watching his back. My love and admiration for him was my biggest inspiration for choosing the path I did.

So when I decided to start my own law firm, it was with the determination that I would help my clients *not* make the same mistakes. Women deserve so much more than to work 60+ hours a week to be paid two-thirds of what a man would make. Female entrepreneurs deserve so much more than to be sued, bankrupted or denied funding in their business for discriminatory reasons.

To escape hustle culture, we have to know how to invest *safely*. How to find outside funding that doesn't put your family's future at risk. How to identify assets you likely already own or have access to, that *could* be paying you passively every single month...if only you knew how.

That is what inspired me to co-author this book with Sarah. I hope you get as much pleasure out of reading it as we did in the writing!

Chapter 1: Why Budgeting Alone Won't Make You Rich

Y ou were told that the first step to financial sovereignty is budgeting. So you tracked your spending. Cut subscriptions. Bought the reusable coffee cup.

But you're still not rich.

That's because budgeting—on its own—won't get you there.

Budgeting is about cutting back. Wealth-building is about expanding your options.

If you've ever felt like you're doing everything "right" but still stuck trading time for money, this chapter will show you why—and what to do instead.

Now, before we get into the *how* it's important that we start with the *why* and aligning our goals. What do YOU want this book to do for you? When we talk about financial goals, many people throw around the word "retirement". Yet as we write this, a recent survey showed that *78% of Americans are behind on saving for retirement.*

So is that really the goal? Most of the time when we talk to a business woman who has little or no retirement plan, her reasoning falls into one of two categories:

1) "My business is my retirement plan," or

2) "I never plan to retire...because I LOVE what I do!"

Well, if you love what you do and don't want to change a thing...why are you reading this book? Seriously.

If you've read this far, it's probably because even though you LOVE what you do, there is something about the way you're doing it that needs to change. If you're like the many business women who come to us for help...you're likely working too many hours and not seeing the results and impact on the world you had hoped for. If you could stop trading time for money and become financially free, you could increase your impact and do more of what you love.

Both the "my business IS my retirement" and the "I never plan to retire" worldviews are symptoms of a major problem with the American retirement system, and it isn't at all surprising that savvy business women are sensing the problem. We generally tend to be intuitive. When our gut and our heart is saying to avoid something, we listen. That's one of the many reasons why women-led companies often outperform predominantly male-led companies in business.

But we're going to challenge your worldview for a minute: what IS this thing Americans call "retirement?"

When you think of retiring, most women tend to think of age 60+, and start listing off a flood of things we always wished we could do but never seemed to get around to: travel, self-care, motivational speaking, charitable work, etc.

Sarah would say that gambling on Wall Street in the hope that you can (perhaps) stop trading time for money when you reach age 65 is a pretty poor financial plan. Funny enough, any investment advisor will be the first to tell you that the traditional retirement strategy doesn't guarantee financial freedom. It's a bit like loading everything you own onto a tiny raft in the middle of the ocean: so long as the economy is calm your boat will have smooth sailing. But the moment the stock market hits a winter storm...your boat is likely to capsize with you in it!

Or, if you're like Sarah when she was 30—maybe you have some vague idea that your business will provide the means for you to retire...without any actual idea of how that will work, fallback plan, or protection against the enormous risk that is entrepreneurship.

Well, if you believe your business can be your retirement plan, we're happy to say you're right! There are five ways a business woman can leverage her company to retire comfortably: three of them involve selling the business and we will be talking about all five in this book.

But what about the woman who wants to stop trading time for money NOW, and not wait until age 65, or a billion-dollar business, to start knocking off that bucket list of dreams?

What if, instead of gambling on Wall Street or giving our best years in an attempt to build a massive business that's really just a gilded cage trapping you in hustle culture...we focused on buying/building assets that paid us passively every month and earned a living without trading time for money?

What if creating wealth in your 20s, 30s and 40s was possible—rather than being a "get rich quick scheme" or a capitalistic scam that gets you ahead on the backs of others...

What if there was a way to do it that benefits the lives you touch, creates greater impact than your business currently ever could, and gives you the time and freedom to give back to your community: by focusing your time and energy on fulfilling your dreams and making the world a better, more beautiful place?

We know all this is possible, because in less than five years Sarah went from working 15+ hour days 7 days a week trading time for money *in her own business*, to living her dream lifestyle on a 16-acre farm.

We both built or bought assets that pay us passively every single day, freeing our time to devote to charity work, travel, hobbies, self-care, church work, and time with family.

We have protections in place so that no matter what happens to either our businesses or our health, our families will be set for life. We have created a life filled solely with work that is meaningful for us; work we would do even if we weren't getting paid—and we can therefore put the funds we earn to work for us in further investments or by giving back.

Following the strategies and mindset shifts we reveal in this book have made it possible for Sarah to fund a charitable movement now spanning 13 countries that brings women's rights to life.

And, it isn't just the two of us who have followed this pathway to financial freedom. Together with our team we have created a movement of radical freedom-seeking women who are doing it too.

This book is about what you need to do to create multiple streams of stable, monthly income in a fool-proof passive way, so you no longer have to trade time for money.

It's about how needle-moving and freeing that process can be, and why some of the most successful and globally recognized entrepreneurs, coaches, mentors, thought leaders, speakers, practitioners, artists and experts have chosen to harness the power of this strategy—to create a life of their own design.

But as well as the 'how-to' and the huge results, this book is also about the roadblocks we see business women and entrepreneurs throw in their own way to obstruct and self-sabotage their progress, the legal mistakes that cost hundreds of thousands in losses, and the oppressive lies and false ideas about money that have been fed to women for thousands of years.

Personally, we hate when someone wastes our time. When we pick up a book, we want to know the author meant to speak to someone like us: in our unique circumstance or with our specific problem. So, to make sure you bought the right book, we will tell you upfront: we wrote this book for three groups of women:

The business woman with an existing successful business who has extra cash at the end of the month, but is afraid of investing, because maybe you've been burned in the past and lost money, or you're hesitating simply because you've NEVER done it before and reinvesting it back into your business has always felt like the safer bet....

If you're not a business owner, but you're very entrepreneurial, maybe you have a side hustle or you are crafty and artsy: you're an author, photographer, artist, or a woman who wishes she could make a bigger impact on the world but has struggled to monetize her passion...

Or, if you're a stay at home mom or WISH you could be a stay at home mom, but the cost of living requires you to work instead of spending time with your kids and fulfilling your desire to give back to your community.

As the founders of a coaching program specializing in helping business women become confident InvestHERs, it is our honor and privilege to share with you *The Fear To Fierce Financial Formula:* a map we have discovered, through our own trial and error, to take you out of the trap of the time-for-money rat race, up to true financial stability and freedom.

The Fear To Fierce Financial Formula

The *Fear To Fierce Financial Formula* is a proven process to take you from a state of fear and financially stuck...

"money is the root of all evil"

"I'm bad with money"

"I can't save."

"I'm ashamed of how much debt I have"

"I'm bad at paying off debt"

...to become financially *fierce* and stably wealthy. The formula contains six steps:

Step 0: Mindset - Strip away false and limiting beliefs that cause you to self-sabotage

Step 1: Profit - Earn more than you spend.

Step 2: Prepare - Ensure you're ready for any disaster or unexpected expense.

Step 3: Eliminate - Pay off debt and build strong credit to eliminate roadblocks to freedom.

Step 4: Protect - Safeguard your assets with financial and legal shields.

Step 5: Grow - Build long-term wealth by focusing on your net worth and creating multiple streams of passive income that exceed your expenses... and then keep going.

In this book, we will focus on showing you one of the most powerful ways to make "Step 1: Profit" a cinch, and then walk you through each step and how to implement it, including adding thousands in monthly passive income, so you can become financially free.

Legal Note: If you have an existing successful business, you may have completed some of the legal protection steps outlined in this book in the past. We recommend reviewing them anyway to *make sure* your wealth is protected. If you have never worked with a business attorney to create a comprehensive legal protection plan for your business, we highly recommend skipping to Chapter 5 and putting those pieces in place *before* you read Chapter 2. And once you have completed all the other steps, do Chapter 5 *again*, directing it at your new investment portfolio and applying the maximizing legal steps in Chapters 5 and 6.

Chapter 2: Scarcity vs Abundance Mindset

S^{*arah*}

What is WEALTH?

If you're going to read an entire book on the subject of building wealth, it's probably a good idea to know what the word means.

But I'm not just asking for a dictionary definition. How do YOU define wealth?

Is wealth running around barefoot on a homestead where you grow your own food?

Or traveling the world eating French croissants and steak dinners?

Maybe wealth is a dollar amount in the bank.

Or time freedom; the ability to do what you please with whom you please whenever you please.

How we define it often comes from the stories we've been taught about money:

Dad: "Money is the root of all evil"

Mom: "I'm bad with money"

Grandpa: "I can't save"

Grandma: "I'm ashamed of how much debt I have"

Broke Uncle: "I'm bad at paying off debt"

Take a moment now to notice what stories you often tell yourself about money and wealth. How do you define wealth and how does the idea of having more of it make you feel?

Here's my favorite definition:

An abundance of valuable possessions or money.

Everyone has a different idea of what "valuable" means. Some people value time, others value family or travel or organic food. But we can all agree that *abundance* is what makes one wealthy or poor. The wealthy have abundance.

Abundance of time.

Abundance of land.

Abundance of food.

Etc.

If a person has loads of cash, cars, and time... but no family, friends or whatever they consider most *valuable* they may consider themselves "poor" despite having a load of money. Because wealth is an abundance of *whatever YOU consider valuable.*

Humanity has often pondered whether money can buy happiness. It doesn't. Money buys *choices* and your choices determine whether or not you're happy. But a woman with no choices is rarely happy... and that's why the definition of wealth includes (for most people) having an abundance of money.

Once you've decided how YOU want to define wealth, the next questions are how do we create wealth, how do we hold onto it once we've got it...and how do we make our money earn us MORE money so we don't have to keep trading our time?

In coaching thousands of women across the US, we have found there are three things that tend to keep business women stuck in "hustle" and hold us back from financial freedom:

Ignorance of the basics of investing, finance, and how to protect themselves

Scarcity mindset, limiting beliefs and fear of investing

Being overwhelmed at the thought of learning how to invest and protect themselves

That is what we will help you overcome in this book, using *The Fear To Fierce Financial Formula.*

The first step of *The Fear To Fierce Financial Formula* is to earn more than you spend. And there are only two ways to do that: you can earn more, or spend less.

Did you have a negative reaction to being told to just "earn more and spend less"?

When most financial advisors talk about building healthy spending habits, they tend to focus on saying "no" to yourself and avoiding activities you enjoy (avocado toast, Starbucks, going to the bar, etc.) in a sort of "I'll suffer now so I can enjoy life later" attitude.

Oftentimes we get this long-suffering mindset about money because we are convinced that hitting a bigger goal (like living your dream lifestyle before age 65) is "impossible".

But what if I told you that **the very fact that you think it is impossible is 99% of the reason you haven't accomplished it yet?**

What you say to yourself becomes your belief. Your beliefs or attitudes can have a profound and very measurable effect on your financial state.

There seem to be two major schools of thought in the business world on the topic of belief.

One set says that focusing on belief is "fluffy" or nonsense, and that DOING is the most important fact in the success of an entrepreneur.

The other half of our world will tell you miraculous stories about folks who have manifested amazing opportunities through things like prayer, meditation, or the power of decision alone.

Each group has converts from the other side...examples and stories to tell; theories and ideas to support each side of this sticky pendulum.

Take Dr. Bruce Moseley, an orthopedic surgeon who, skeptical of all the talk on "mind over matter," was forced to admit the validity of some part of it after he noticed a placebo group responded as well to being told they had been operated on as his actual patients did!

"But Sarah: is just thinking positively REALLY enough to fix my money problems?"

Yes!

In his book The Anatomy of Hope, Dr. Jerome Groopman stated:

"Researchers are learning that a change in mindset has the power to alter neurochemistry. Belief and expectation - the key elements of hope - can block pain by releasing the brain's endorphins and enkephalins, mimicking the effect of morphine."

And in the 1980s, clinical psychologist Dr. Alfred Barrios conducted a series of tests to determine whether geniuses are BORN or MADE.

Barrios wanted to know: "Can anyone be a genius?"

He published the results of his research in a 1980 article of the *National Enquirer* where he said:

"Most people have the mistaken idea that geniuses are born, not made...These are traits that anyone can develop. It makes no difference how old you are, how much education you have, or what you have accomplished to date."

His 24 characteristics of genius included such things as drive, outgoingness, optimism, courage, imagination, and willingness to take chances.

And in his clinic, he proved that anyone can operate at genius level if they successfully adopt these characteristics!

In other words, what we often think of as our "personality" is really just our habits.

I remember at the beginning of 2023 when I first began my TikTok channel. My intention was to educate women on how easy it is to go from a hustler to an InvestHER when you buy or build cash flowing assets and begin earning passive income every month.

The first video I ever had go viral was a 7-second pan of my farm with a text overlay that simply said:

Stop chasing.

Chasing money

Chasing success

Chasing people

Get yourself a 16-acre farm. Grow hay and sell it, AirBnb the farmhouse, rent out the field as a wedding venue, host wellness retreats, and just... live happily

That video got 9k views, 267 likes, was saved 63 times, and received 30 comments. But what amazed me the most was this: *nearly every comment was a sarcastic, I-can't-be-lieve-you're-this-dumb,* trolling-type rebuttal!

Now, a small percentage of those people were likely of a category I like to call "haters": nasty, little weasel types whose lives begin and end with scrolling the Internet looking for ways to put down, invalidate and generally destroy all the good in the world. Such people exist (you're a business owner: you know!) but they are a tiny percentage of the population.

So when a LARGE percentage of people get sarcastic or trolling on my posts, the experienced business owner in me pays attention. These people aren't haters. They are everyday business women who are hurting. Feeling trapped by a broken financial system...and their sarcastic comments of disbelief are often a plea to be proven wrong.

As a Certified Life Coach with 15 years of experience in coaching and spiritual counseling, I got to work using my coaching tools to understand better what my audience needed from me. After responding to a few comments and having longer conversations in DM's and a few 1:1 Zoom calls, it became clear:

The one thing all the people I spoke to had in common was a scarcity mindset.

Oh, there were a few grateful, kind or encouraging comments, too! But when I tallied it all up (as we data-driven entrepreneurs like to do), the largest percentage had a common thread: *I could never afford to do this.*

Possibly on your current income and budget that seems very true of some of your own InvestHER goals, too.

If so, this scarcity mindset is exactly why you're stuck right where you are. So I'm going to let you in on a little secret:

Today, I live on a 16-acre farm that I first manifested (postulated, dreamed of and had no idea how to make happen) just three years ago.

The craziest part of all this is that the 7-second video was based on my everyday life. I was simply naming the passive income streams that have earned us $10k after investing in an asset (our farm) less than two years ago.

Today, because of this and several other assets I have bought or built that earn me passive income every month, I am able to devote time to public speaking, writing, hobbies, travel, spiritual retreats, family and giving back to my community through charitable giving, volunteering, fundraising and coaching.

I can do this because I own assets that deliver enormous value in exchange for my income, without demanding my time.

All those sarcastic "get real," "that would never work," "sounds nice but I could never afford it" type comments came from women who honestly believed they could never make this happen!

And yet...what all those doubters failed to realize was: my life and financial situation was a whole lot worse than most people just five years ago.

It was May 2018. I had walked away from my former life in LA with no real plan of what would come next. My husband, Ben, and I had $500 in the bank and his beat up 1988 Toyota 4Runner. We slept in that truck, homeless, for two weeks, and then crashed at my little brother's house for a few months afterwards. I was 31-years-old. I had built and sold a successful business a decade before, but had no income now, barely any savings left, and had never invested a dime of my money.

That was only five years ago. If I can come this far in so little time, is it possible for others to do the same? What is the difference between me and those who fail to accomplish their financial freedom goals?

There are many possible answers to that, and we cannot discount privilege, my business background, and the friend who cared enough to sit me down at age 30 and explain how investing works. Without him, none of this would have been possible.

But, when I looked at those doubting and sarcastic comments, it dawned on me that there was one thing that set me apart from them. One important thing. But most importantly: one thing YOU, dear reader, can actually do to increase your chances of success.

I believed it was possible.

What you say to yourself becomes your belief. Changing your beliefs can alter your chances of achieving financial success *because it forces you to look for answers and solutions you would not have seen if you believed no solution was possible.*

What we often think of as our "personality" is really just our habits.

Positive inner dialogue is mainly about exercising your mental "muscles" until you can bring about a positive outlook toward situations and your own future potential.

Oh sure, there were strategies I later learned that allowed me to buy or build assets that pay me passively each month. There were coaches whose secrets I availed myself of, and mentors whose wisdom and support made all this possible.

But, in the beginning, I didn't have any of that. What I DID have was a burning, obsessive desire to achieve financial freedom and devout, unshakable CERTAINTY that it was possible.

I was so determined, so irrevocably *sure* that it was possible that I ignored all naysayers, doubters and haters in my life (of whom there were many) and figured out how to do it anyway.

How I learned to be that positive is a long story I will delve into in a later chapter. Here the important thing to understand is the difference between *scarcity vs abundance mindset.*

A scarcity mindset tells you that financial freedom is limited to a few privileged individuals. That there is a finite amount of money or success to be had in the world and to get it you must take it away from somebody else.

Scarcity mindset believes financial freedom is undesirable. That it is evil to want more than you have (you should absolutely practice gratitude without allowing it to cripple your very natural desire to want more) and believing that what you have now is all you will ever have.

Scarcity mindset tells you who you are today is a product of your "DNA" or "genes" or "generational curses" not *the truth which is that who you are today is a product of your decisions and the attitudes and beliefs you accepted as "truth" far more than the experiences you believe shaped them.*

It is not that your past experiences (or present circumstance) cannot affect you. Your experiences can either fuel you or consume you. I often share the parable with my clients of the two brothers: one is a successful and ambitious businessman. The other is a homeless beggar. When asked why they ended up where they are today, both say, "Because my father was an alcoholic."

If scarcity mindset could be summed up as the idea that you *can't* accomplish your goals, financial or otherwise, (due to some inherent mental, spiritual, physical or financial lack or disability) or that it is impossible without stealing success from somebody else, what then is abundance mindset?

Abundance mindset is summed up in two distinct phrases:

1) the soul-deep belief that financial success is not a privilege: it is a duty,

and 2) an equally heartfelt certainty that your potential for success and wealth is limitless IF you apply the principle of *giving greater than expected value in exchange for money.*

To understand this, you must first understand what money actually is. Throughout history it has taken many forms: coins, gems, stamped pieces of leather...and today we have things like cryptocurrency that do not even exist except as computer code!

But money itself is none of those things.

"Money has worth because for most people it represents something valuable."

Investopedia

All money, no matter its form, is purely and simply a *symbol of value*. And that is why the potential for wealth is infinite: because you are not a rock. Or dirt. Or a piece of meat. Or some other inanimate object. You are a living, thinking being with the potential for limitless invention and imagination...in other words, limitless ability to *provide value* to society.

That is also why money itself is not the root of evil. Many people believe the Bible says this, but in actual fact most translations of the Bible (including the King James Version) state that *"love of money is the root of all evil"*. Which just furthers my point!

To say money *itself* is the root of evil is like saying the written word is the root of all evil! Words are merely symbols. So is money. It is the *intention* and *meaning* behind words that make them good or bad. When you love money more than the people who gave it to you, you often tend to give poor value in exchange for it. It is the *value* exchanged for money that makes your money evil or benign.

One could steal from banks or deal drugs to drum up cash: both acts have negative value to society and, therefore, they are evil. You could also invent a cure for cancer and exchange it with every doctor and patient around the world as a very positive value in exchange for money.

If money is simply a symbol for the *value* you have brought to the world...can you see why financial success is not a privilege: it is a duty?

But, if money really is *nothing but a symbol for the value you bring the world*, why then are some of the most incredibly valuable, caring, hard-working entrepreneurs in the world...utterly broke?

Well, one reason is because they often believe money is undesirable. Scarcity mindset makes them give away their time or give value and ask nothing in return. Don't get me wrong: I do charitable work all the time. In fact, I have personally volunteered more than 10,000 hours of my time to various nonprofit organizations in the past 15 years! Volunteerism is a lovely thing...when your own financial needs are being met. But, when it is done to the point of starvation, it usually stems from a scarcity mindset.

Then there are the people who have criminal tendencies. Out of insanity or ignorant desperation, they obsess over the symbol "money" and try to obtain it without offering value in return. Their success or failure to do so makes the subject seem dirty...and obscures the fact that financial success is a duty by making it *appear* to be an evil act.

Actually, it is only the desire to pervert the symbol (money) by removing the *value* it was supposed to represent that is truly evil.

So fear or disgust at the idea of having abundance are the first barriers to building wealth.

Your ability to dream up, think up, invent, or imagine *value* you can offer to others in exchange for wealth is what makes your potential for financial success limitless. And it is also what makes escaping hustle and becoming an InvestHER an ethical thing to do, as it frees up your time to do more good and have a greater impact on the world.

***

Let's Reflect On This

Start a 30-day journal to document the limiting beliefs and negative attitudes you currently have about money and investing. What stories are you telling yourself that trigger fear or other negative emotions at the thought of chasing after your dreams?

Once you have identified a few of them, begin exercising self-discipline to reframe those thoughts to a higher-vibe belief or thought.

Keep a note on your phone or a small notepad and pen in your pocket throughout the day.

Every time you start to worry or experience negative emotions or thoughts about your goals and dreams, pause and make a note of it.

When you see an opportunity, do you get excited? Or does your mind tell you, *"You're not good enough. You'll never be able to accomplish that!"* Etc.?

Each time you think a negative thought about your goal, make a conscious effort to stop yourself.

Focusing on that specific thought, flip the script and put your *intention* behind thinking positively about it. This can be verbal or nonverbal.

Examples:

If my limiting belief is: "I can't do this," I rephrase it like this: "I am infinitely capable of accomplishing my goals. Not only *can* I do it... I AM doing it every...single...day."

If my negative thought is: "I'll never hit $1M dollars," I pause, and consciously reframe that thought as: "By the end of next year, I will be a $1M business owner."

In 2013, the Canadian Psychological Association published a study called, *The Efficacy and Effectiveness of Psychological Treatments,* where they announced:

"These therapies work as well as or better than drugs for depression, anxiety, obsessive-compulsive disorder, and post-traumatic stress disorder;".

By thinking positively, you can not only alter your neurochemistry, but form new beliefs that influence your attitude, and therefore, the outcome of all your financial endeavors.

Document in your journal which forms of self-care (preventative mental wellness) are effective for you, and which of your daily activities are most harmful to your mental health.

Chapter 3: Retirement Is Dead

S *arah*

Most entrepreneurial women in America are following a retirement plan that was never designed for them.

In fact, it was never meant for business owners at all—and certainly not for women who crave time freedom, financial independence, and a life of our own design. The traditional retirement model is failing us, and in this chapter, I'll show you why...and what to do instead.

My Wake-Up Call

In 2019, I got a call from my friend Cary Green—now the co-founder of Green Era Financial. "I just got licensed as a financial advisor and need someone to practice on. Would you help me as a friend?"

I said yes. Cary and I had been through a lot together, and I trusted he wouldn't waste my time. I didn't know it then, but this call would completely change how I saw my future.

He asked me questions about my spending, how much I made at my job and the weekend wedding business I had started earlier that year. After taking thorough notes, he showed me his screen and concluded: "Here's what you would need to invest each month in order to retire comfortably by age 65." I felt the blood rush to my face.

"*$1,200 a month!?*" I looked back at him, "That's insane!"

To be honest, I felt betrayed. I knew I was behind, but that seemed like a really high number. Heck, I knew plenty of other successful $6+figure business women, and few of them had that kind of extra cash either!

"Who has that kind of extra money?" I asked incredulously.

Cary rubbed the back of his neck, sheepish. "Well, most people start a lot younger, so they don't have to invest so much."

"I'm only 30, Cary." I gave him side-eye. "Are you calling me old?"

"No!" He shrugged, "Didn't your old jobs have benefits?"

They did, but I hadn't worked at a corporate job very long. I thought back to all those years when I had money, but spent it or kept reinvesting it back into my business...because isn't that what you're supposed to do?

That moment planted a seed: *Maybe retirement is different for business owners.*

A New Model Emerges

Fast forward eight months. My wedding business was thriving, and I was still working a corporate job I liked—but something was stirring. One day, I sat in on a client workshop hosted by Eric Miller, co-founder of Econologics®, who specialised in advising private healthcare business owners.

His talk was titled: **"Why The Traditional Retirement Plan Is Not For Practice Owners."**

Eric explained: "The traditional model is built for employees. It's based on how much you can accumulate in savings accounts, 401(k)s, IRAs, or brokerage accounts—so you can one day stop working at a job."

He paused. "But that model isn't for business owners. It was never meant for you."

My brain lit up like a firework show.

Suddenly, I understood why Cary's advice had felt like trying to jam a round peg into a square hole. It wasn't that I was behind or irresponsible. I was just using the wrong formula.

As Eric outlined five options available only to business owners—ways to skip the traditional "retirement" path and build **Financial Freedom** instead (when your monthly passive income exceeds your expenses)—everything clicked.

I already had the asset I needed: my business. It could become my retirement plan.

Destiny

If you're like me, the concept that your retirement can be based, NOT just upon the money you accumulate over time in your savings accounts, but how you choose to build your business (and business income sources such as passive income) is probably blowing your mind!

Before I left the big national law firm (where I worked five solid years on the hamster wheel), I was completely under the impression that I needed to SAVE every dime into my 401k for retirement. This was despite knowing – deep down – that I was NOT going to stay at that job my whole life and that I was an entrepreneur at heart. I was there to learn the law and I learned it well at that firm.

But you know what they DIDN'T teach? Real retirement advice for someone who wants to go into business for themselves. Honestly, I am not sure where they teach this – because I had never really heard of this until (fast forward) the first financial consultation I had with Sarah (yes, the Sarah in this book) just this last year.

I can remember her saying –

"Well, your retirement, that will be your business."

It sounded so casual, but it hit me hard. No one had ever said that to me before.

I grew up thinking that retirement meant saving diligently, putting everything into a 401(k), and hoping for the best. My dad did the opposite—he built and sold businesses, and then reinvested into real estate. I used to think he was doing it all wrong... until I realised *he was the example I needed*.

If I hadn't learned this from Sarah, I would've left my Big Law job and started my practice with zero strategy for achieving financial freedom. I would've just traded one hustle for another.

Now, as co-founder of our coaching business and CEO of Bounds Law, I'm building intentionally—so that my business supports me *even when I'm not working in it*. And that's what I want for every woman reading this.

Because it's not about just owning a business. It's about *building a business that builds your freedom*.

The Myth We've Been Sold

Sarah

So how did we get here? Why do so many of us feel stuck in a system that doesn't serve us?

For the history nerds like me—here's what *really* happened.

Let's start with this: if we adjust for inflation, Americans today are making less than our great-grandparents did during the Great Depression.

According to the IRS, the average annual income in 1930 was around $4,800. That's nearly $85,000 in today's dollars.

Now? The current average income for a single American is only $56,000.

That's a nearly $30,000 gap.

We are living through what economists are calling a **Silent Depression.** Wages are down. Expenses are up. Housing, food, childcare—it's all higher than ever. And yet we're still being fed the same retirement advice our grandparents got.

This isn't just flawed. It's a scam.

Let's take it back to the turn of the century...

The year is 1904. You're a working-class woman in Detroit. You and your friends gather on Sundays to sew, chat, and swap stories. Henry Ford just opened a new factory on Piquette Avenue. Your town is buzzing.

You land a job there—steady pay, decent hours. By 1914, Ford starts offering pensions to employees who stick with the company for decades. It feels revolutionary. Your daughter eventually joins you as one of Ford's secretaries.

By 1935, President Roosevelt signs the Social Security Act. Retirement age is officially set at 65.

Sounds great, right?

Here's the kicker: in 1935, **the average life expectancy was just 62.**

Let that sink in.

The retirement plan was a brilliant political move—**because most Americans didn't live long enough to collect it.**

It wasn't created to support the people. It was created to keep the people happy being little cogs in the wheel.

Fast forward: the middle class grows. Medical science improves. People start living longer. And suddenly—those pensions? They start costing corporations *a lot* more money.

Enter: the 401(k).

In 1978, banks and Wall Street firms convinced the government to let them package retirement into a neat, fee-generating financial product. Corporations loved it because they no longer had to fund retirements. Banks loved it because they got to manage your money *and* charge you for it. And the American people?

We were sold a dream. Again.

If you earned enough, saved enough, and stayed in one job for 40 years, *maybe* you'd retire in comfort.

But what about entrepreneurs? Freelancers? Women who left the workforce to raise kids?

What about the ones who didn't get employer matches? Or the ones whose salaries never stretched far enough to save?

They were—and still are—left behind.

So here we are.

Corporate profits are at an all-time high. Wages are stagnant. Inflation is soaring. And most women I work with are still being told that a 401(k) and hope are their best bet at financial freedom.

The Truth About Financial Freedom for Successful Business Women

Here's the truth: **the fastest and most reliable path to financial freedom as a female entrepreneur isn't gambling your hard-earned money in the stock market.** It's learning to *leverage the most valuable asset you already own*—your business—to build wealth and passive income on your terms.

When people say *"your business is your retirement plan,"* they're right. But it's not because you should reinvest every dime back into your business in the hope that this ONE income stream will support you forever. And it's certainly not an all-or-nothing bet that you'll one day magically get an offer to buy you out right when you need it.

It's because your business is a sum of *assets*: ones that can be leveraged, sold, automated, or licensed to create **passive income**.

This isn't a dig at the stock market. Think of it this way: If you were a real estate investor with five beautifully maintained rental properties—but they were all sitting empty—would you:

a) Rush out to buy another property, or

b) Focus on getting tenants into the homes you already own?

Obviously, it would make more sense to start by *monetizing the assets you ALREADY own.*

And yet, many business owners overlook the untapped wealth sitting inside their own business—their knowledge, frameworks, and client results, and jump headfirst into unfamiliar investments—like crypto or stocks—because that's what they've been told "smart investors" do.

Your business IS the basis of your retirement plan. But not just any business. A business built intentionally—with systems, teams, and most importantly: by monetizing the magic that makes your business function... in a way that earns without you at the center of it.

When you do that, you're no longer chained to the hustle. You can:

Travel and enjoy life more freely

Spend time with family or focus on your health

Hire a CEO and step away from day-to-day operations

Reinvest your profits into other wealth-building assets (including stocks, crypto or real estate if you wish)

Or sell your business—partially or fully—for long-term retirement

That's what financial sovereignty looks like.

Chapter 4: What Intellectual Property Really Is—and Why It Matters

S^{arah}

You carry within you an asset more precious than gold. Your zone of genius. It's the collection of your stories, wisdom, and gifts—shaped by your life, your lessons, and your hard-won experience. Destiny would call this intellectual property:

Intellectual Property: *a work or invention that is the result of creativity, such as a manuscript or a design, to which one has rights and for which one may apply for a patent, copyright, trademark, etc.*

I call it your magic.

You were raised in a world that taught you to hustle—to believe that value must be measured by the hour, by your effort, by your constant presence. But what if your truest value isn't bound by time at all? What if your greatest investment isn't a stock or a piece of real estate—but the transformation you can deliver through your voice, your systems, your lived experience?

In this chapter, we'll help you see what's already within your grasp: **your magic is your greatest asset.** We'll explore why it matters—not just for building wealth, but for discovering your basic purpose, increasing your impact, and your ability to create life on your own terms. Because when you harness magic, you don't just boost your revenue—you craft financial freedom.

Your intellectual property—your experience, your expertise, your original ideas—is the most overlooked and underleveraged wealth-building opportunity available to you. It's the foundation of what I call your "magic."

Magic, in this context, isn't about spells or potions. It's the unique value you bring to the table. It's your voice, your stories, your processes, your client transformations, your hard-won lessons. And when you learn how to monetize that magic, you unlock a form of wealth-building that isn't just profitable—it's liberating.

Most women have been conditioned to believe that the only way to earn money is to trade their time for it. That's the hustle script. And for a while, it works—until it doesn't. Until your time runs out. Until you burn out. Until you look up and realize you've built a business that depends entirely on your availability.

That's where I was.

When I built my wedding business in Portland, I was working 15-hour weekends and 40-hour weeks. I loved what I did—but the lifestyle? It was unsustainable. My husband, Ben, who thrives on adventure and weekend hikes, asked me one day if I'd ever be willing to slow down. That question changed everything.

I started looking for ways to leverage my decade of experience in the wedding industry without tying it to my time. I created an online course to teach couples how to plan their own weddings, using my magic—my experiences, proven method, and insights. Within months, I was making more than double what I used to, and working a fraction of the hours. If you dig a level deeper...what I had done was flip the script on how I *thought* about monetizing my expertise.

This chapter is your invitation to make the same shift.

Let's start by reframing how we think about value. Most people believe that value = time. But that's not true. Value is about transformation. If you can help someone solve a painful problem or reach an aspirational goal, the time it takes you to deliver that result is irrelevant. In fact, the faster you can help someone achieve transformation, the *more* valuable your offer becomes.

Yet often when women think about monetizing their knowledge, skills and experience, their first thought is to find (or create in the case of a side hustle or business) a *job*. In other words, they trade their time for money.

This isn't because the natural order of the universe is to trade time for money—it's because *you've been indoctrinated to believe your time is the only thing of value you have to offer.* From a young age, you were probably asked what you wanted to be when you grew up. The "correct" answers were always professions—doctor, teacher, lawyer. Rarely was the answer a dream, a vision, or even "a strong independent woman."

That mindset conditioned many of us to tie our worth to what we spend the most *time* doing. And it's why so many women end up in businesses that consume every ounce of their energy.

Yet this is what makes intellectual property so powerful. When you package your ideas, processes, or frameworks into a product—whether that's a course, a system, or a method—you create something that can deliver transformation over and over again, without requiring your involvement.

In chapter 2, I said this is the ethical path to wealth: deliver more value than you receive in return, and do so in a way that doesn't depend on you showing up every single day.

That's the core principle of what I call the Passive Income Pathway Method.

Here's how to start putting it into practice:

Step 1: Make a list of your magic.

What are you great at? What do people constantly ask you for help with? What do your clients thank you for again and again? These are not random talents—they're clues to your intellectual property.

Step 2: Choose one spark of magic and dissect it.

Ask yourself: *What transformation does this create? What framework, story, or method do I use to deliver that result?* That clarity is the beginning of turning an invisible strength into a tangible asset.

Step 3: Stop thinking like a Worker Bee and start thinking like an InvestHER.

When a Worker Bee sees something that needs to be done, her first thought is: *"How do I squeeze that onto my to-do list?"*

When a LeadHER Bee sees something to be done, her first thought is: *"How do I hire or pay someone to do this?"*

But when an InvestHER sees something to be done, her first thought is: *"Who has what I need, and needs what I have?"* **Because if you can answer that, you can create partnerships where someone pays YOU for the privilege of taking the task off your plate.**

Read that sentence again. People will pay you to take work off your plate—if you package and protect your IP.

This is why intellectual property is the entrepreneur's fastest, most reliable pathway to wealth. Not because you keep reinvesting back into a time-hungry business model, but because you use contract law—and occasionally automation—to deliver value to the masses without tying it to your hours.

And this isn't theory—it's happening everywhere.

In 2003, J.K. Rowling was reported to have become wealthier than Queen Elizabeth II. *But it wasn't through selling Harry Potter books!*

Today, she earns $95 million per year from companies like Disney, Walmart...and their British equivalents: companies that pay Big Bucks for the privilege of doing work FOR her: designing costumes, wands, movies, etc., based on her IP.

Michael Jordan is the most iconic and famous basketball player of all time. He is also a self-made billionaire. But not from playing basketball. Jordan earns $256 million per year licensing his name to Nike for the honor and privilege of *manufacturing shoes & other swag for him.*

But you don't need to be a famous celebrity to use this strategy for passive income.

Destiny Bounds earns 17% of every sale I make of our online course *Confident InvestHER Academy,* which includes 7 lessons she recorded and licensed to me to help InvestHERs understand her Legal Roadmap Method to protect their wealth, and will (of course) earn additional royalties from the sale of this book.

At the time of this writing, roughly half of my monthly bills are paid every month by passive income, and it is how I have been able to go from ZERO savings, retirement plans or investments at age 30, to being on track to retire by the time I'm 45.

This is the power of monetizing your magic.

And in the next chapters, we'll show you exactly how to do it, too.

Chapter 5: Finding Your Magic

S *arah*

By now, you understand why your intellectual property—your magic—is your greatest asset. But at this point, most women fall into one of two camps: either you're thinking, *"I don't have any IP worth leveraging,"* or you're overwhelmed with ideas and can't figure out which one to monetize first.

Let me show you how I help women *find your magic.*

Step 1: Brainstorm every result you've created.

I'll often start by asking women to tell me stories. What were some of the best results you've gotten for your clients? What problems have you solved in your own life or business that others still struggle with? As she talks, I listen for the threads—repeatable processes, proven frameworks, surprising outcomes. These stories are the raw material of your IP.

Step 2: Differentiate between the *value* and the *time*.

Sometimes it's difficult for women to dissect how their magic is valuable without their presence. After a lifetime of indoctrination, and years or perhaps decades of tying your *own worth* to time (charging by the hour, delivering your modality hands-on, etc) it can feel like mental gymnastics to dissect your expertise.

But once the stories are on the table, we pull them apart. This is where my *A–Z Framework* comes in. We identify point **A**—where the client was before applying her magic—and point **Z**—the specific transformation. This shift helps the entrepreneur see that the true value lies not in the hours she worked, but in the *change* she created. Often this is the first time she realizes, "Oh—I don't have to sell my time. I can sell this result."

Note: Occasionally, the most powerful IP lies not in the results gotten for clients, but the internal processes or SOPs inside the business itself. An example of this is my Million-Dollar Hiring Method. I built an incredible team within my own business using 7 "filters" not typically included in the hiring process, to hone in on the best candidates without wasting my (or their) time. This isn't something I was *selling* to clients. It was an internal process I developed for myself, that helped us build a highly efficient and profitable team. Once I dissected that magic and packaged it up, it became just another asset I could use for passive income.

Step 3: Break it into milestones.

Transformation rarely happens in one giant leap; it's a path of smaller steps. Together, we map out the journey between A and Z. What were the turning points? What made the difference? Each milestone becomes a building block of her method. And when we give those milestones names, the method gains structure, clarity, and most importantly—instant perceived value.

Step 4: Name and protect your method.

Finally, I ask her to name it. Giving your method a title isn't about ego—it's ownership. It makes it possible for us to protect the work in the eyes of the law. From there, we ensure the IP can be protected through trademark, copyright, or even patent. Destiny will cover that further in the next chapter. This step ensures that your brilliance isn't just a loose idea; it's an asset you can claim, defend, and monetize.

Case Studies:

Jennifer—Too Many Ideas, Not Enough Clarity

When Jennifer came to me, she already knew she had powerful expertise to share. Her challenge wasn't a lack of IP—it was too much of it. She was trying to cram several offers into one, which made her transformation statement vague and uncompelling to potential collaborators. Using the A–Z Framework, we dissected her expertise into specific, high-value problems she solved in a unique way. The result? A trademarkable method that became the foundation for a $10k offer, ready to be leveraged into passive income.

Dr. Aversa—"I Don't Have Any Magic"

Dr. Aversa, a healthcare provider with over a decade of experience, came to me convinced she had no IP worth monetizing. Imposter syndrome had her doubting everything. By walking her through my brainstorm process, I helped her uncover her true zone of genius—unique insights and systems she'd been using with clients for years. We packaged it into her first digital product, which she's now able to license to partners in her industry. What once felt like "nothing special" became her ticket to scalable wealth.

Chapter 6: Protecting Your Magic

D^{estiny}

In 2022, a survey was done of Millennials and Gen Zers, asking those who were behind on retirement what their strategy was to catch up. The survey came back with two results:

Win the lottery

Sue a rich person

We will not comment on the massive failure of our educational system which led the younger generations into thinking THAT is their only hope for financial freedom...

...but instead focus on the fact that: *if we are going to help you become financially independent we had better make sure you have a plan in place for protecting that wealth from everybody who isn't.*

So, your next step is to protect your newly-discovered IP assets from those who are too lazy or too stupid to earn their own money and would rather just take yours!

In order to understand the two tools we use for protection, first, you will need to understand a couple of basic legal terms:

Liability: the state of being legally responsible for something.

For example: *By renting out her home, Suzie was **liable** for the medical bills when her tenant came in drunk, tripped over his own feet, and broke his arm.*

Another example: *By creating an online course teaching children how to knit, Ann was **liable** for the damages when a toddler, left unattended with the knitting needles, used them to stab holes in her mother's couch.*

Are you beginning to see why understanding liability is important?

The moment we buy or build an asset, such as a rental property, and begin to earn passive income, we also collect potential *liabilities*. Scenarios where we are legally (and financially) responsible for something.

So, how do you get rid of liability? How do you invest safely...or at least, lower your risk of being held liable for someone else's mistakes or stupid decisions?

Pro Tip: I want to clarify one VERY important thing for this book - your "business" could also be in the non-traditional sense such as rental properties, investment type accounts, even that Uber or DoorDash driver, and other side hustles that simply bring you money NOT from a W-2. The government, for good or bad, considers this "business" income and the law WILL consider you a "business" if anything ever goes wrong. In other words, you can be sued directly for your work if you're making that money outside of your W-2 job. The law does not give "freebies" to business owners who plead ignorance that they "weren't one."

So, how do we business owners protect ourselves?

This brings me to my *Legal Protection RoadMap* for putting your business in tip-top legal shape.

As discussed previously, we are going to assume that you have done this on your initial business already, and are now just trying to add additional sources of passive income.

First, you will want to ensure you have the proper legal entity in place (and no, "sole proprietor" is NOT a "legal" entity nor does it provide any protection to you personally). This could also include adding additional legal entities or converting your legal entity to something more beneficial to your needs.

Secondly, you will want to ensure that you have contracts and agreements in place that LIMIT your liability. These provisions will also change as your income sources change and your risk level increases.

You might be thinking – I don't have any contracts or agreements that I need. I promise, over the last decade, these "contracts" and "agreements" can come in so many different forms such as "terms and conditions," "invoices," "receipts," "bill of sale," or even just a "ticket" that has terms on the back. The language in these agreements can be super crucial if an accident or injury occurs within your business, investment property, or while earning 1099 income.

Third, business insurance is a MUST and ensuring you have the proper coverage type and amount can be critical if someone sues or even threatens to sue you.

Fourth, ensure that your business meets all regulatory and compliance requirements.

Last, it is vitally important that you protect your business's LARGEST asset, your intellectual property. We will get into this more in later chapters, but your IP is TRULY one of your greatest business resources when it comes to achieving financial freedom. Not only do you want to protect this, you will soon learn that this can be one of your biggest passive income streams.

So, how do these things REALLY protect us and our business?

The purpose of legal entities, contracts, terms & conditions, etc., is to *limit* your liability.

The purpose of insurance is to *transfer* your liability to the insurance company (someone else), giving you peace of mind.

The purpose of trademarks, copyright law, patents, etc., is to *secure* your intellectual property so no one can steal it or use it without your permission (and profit).

Let's explore how that works:

In the example earlier, Suzie's tenant got drunk, then tripped over nothing and hurt himself while renting her property. If she has worked with an attorney to create proper contracts, her liability for medical bills could be *limited* to a certain amount, or possibly even *transferred* entirely to the tenant himself.

If Suzie worked with an insurance agent, she probably also has liability insurance in place. That means even if her tenant decides to dispute the contract he signed and sue her, and for some reason he wins, her insurance company will pay the bill...not Suzie.

In our other example, Ann is a knitting expert and created an online course and automated sales process that brings her monthly passive income. One of her students decided to leave their toddler unattended with the knitting needles and used them to stab holes in a couch, and the parent demands a refund or threatens to sue. Ann has worked with an attorney, so the parent already accepted the Terms & Conditions of the course, which should *transfer* or *limit* her liability for these types of damages. She also has Errors & Omissions Insurance, so even if a court finds that she omitted to warn parents about the dangers of knitting needles, her insurance company is liable for the damages...not Ann.

In both cases, it's important to note that Ann and Suzie are both good, ethical people and might choose to pay the medical bills, or replace the mother's couch, as an act of goodwill and kindness. But they will not be *forced* to do so by the legal system out of lack of financial and legal protection!

We already stated in the first chapter that Sarah and I strongly believe that earning passive income is ONLY ethical (and indeed financial success is a duty) if we earn it by *delivering value far in excess of the money received.*

These tools can be abused, and indeed have been many times, by unethical business owners and investors who give capitalism a very bad name. They use contracts, terms &

conditions, or insurance *to get away with taking no responsibility for things they are very much responsible for!*

I want no such behavior to ever be considered acceptable by my clients, students of my courses, or you, my dear reader. We use these tools ONLY and SOLELY to protect ourselves from unethical, scammy, greedy people. People who purposely "fall" and pretend to be hurt, or careless parents who leave their toddler unattended with sharp objects and then seek to blame someone else for the result.

So, those are the hard facts of the matter. Taking these four steps before you begin to invest will go far in reducing your investment risk and make it much more likely that you will achieve financial freedom.

Chapter 7: More About Legal Protection of Your Wealth

*S*arah

    This chapter may feel like a detour from our topic of "*how to monetize your magic*", but I assure you it is not! After all, what is the point of creating passive income if you take shortcuts that harm your business or your family... or lead to lawsuits, lengthy court battles, etc?

So to save you from heartache and financial loss, both Destiny and I will delve deep into our own magic in this chapter to ensure you have proper asset protection and risk management strategies in place before you begin to create your first passive income stream.

Estate Planning with IP

Dying too early is the most expensive thing you can do, and your family pays the price. I know that is a morbid way to begin a paragraph...but hear me out:

As a financial strategist and money coach for business women, one of the most heart-breaking parts of my job is dealing with my clients' finances when she passes away.

It doesn't happen often...thank God.

But I've witnessed this enough times to know what happens when a business woman's financial planning is done RIGHT...and when it is not.

Statistically speaking, one study showed in 2022 that **only 16.4% of family-owned businesses survive the unexpected death of the owner.**

If you're like me...you probably started your business out of a passion to serve your community! And more so when you begin to monetize your intellectual property. If your family, employees and others rely on that income, you don't want your passive income stream to die with you. Therefore, we MUST put proper protections in place.

The right person to help you create an Estate Plan is an attorney.

Destiny

What happens to your wealth if you pass away unexpectedly?

The answer depends on whether or not you have created an Estate Plan.

Estate Plan: the process of anticipating and arranging for the management and disposal of a person's estate during the person's life in preparation for a person's future incapacity or death.

Studies suggest that around 60% of American adults don't have a will or any form of estate plan. This is particularly prevalent among younger generations. Even though COVID did improve these numbers, they are still staggeringly high, for business owners especially.

And as business owners, it is even *more* devastating if something happens to you without an estate plan in place. Not only is your family impacted, but your employees, your clients and sometimes even the community your business serves can be hurt by the loss of you and/or your business.

So, before you even think about leveraging your IP, Step 4 of *The Fear To Fierce Financial Formula* includes asking yourself the question – *what will happen to what I build if I pass unexpectedly?*

Remember Sarah's story concerning the doctor who was suddenly hospitalized? This truly happens more frequently than you can imagine.

If you can't confidently say that you know what will happen to your business, your employees, your clients and your family if you die tomorrow, you do NOT have a proper estate plan in place.

Estate planning is an essential facet of securing your hard-earned wealth and assets for the future. It encompasses a series of crucial decisions and legal preparations aimed at ensuring your estate is managed and distributed according to your wishes after you pass away.

What exactly does estate planning entail?

It involves more than just drafting a will. Estate planning encompasses various elements such as wills, trusts, powers of attorney, healthcare directives, and beneficiary designations (deciding who would own your assets when you die). Make sure that when you are talking to an attorney about your future planning needs, each of these are discussed.

Here are the common components of Estate Planning so you can be prepared:

Will: A will is a fundamental document that outlines how your assets will be distributed among beneficiaries after your death. It also designates guardianship for minor children, if applicable.

Trusts: Trusts can offer more control over how assets are distributed, potentially avoiding probate and providing flexibility in managing assets.

Powers of Attorney: These documents designate individuals to make financial and healthcare decisions on your behalf if you become incapacitated.

Healthcare Directives: Also known as a living will, this outlines your preferences for medical treatment if you are unable to communicate your wishes.

Beneficiary Designations: Ensuring beneficiaries are updated on accounts like life insurance policies, retirement plans, and bank accounts is crucial for a smooth transfer of assets.

Buy/Sell Agreements: A contract between business partners which controls the re-assignment of a share of a business in the event that a partner dies or is unable to continue working.

Why are these important? Here is a bit more information on what each of these will do or prevent for you:

Will: Provides clear instructions for asset distribution and guardianship.

Trusts: Offer control over asset management and can potentially reduce estate taxes and avoid probate.

Powers of Attorney: Essential for decision-making if you're unable to do so.

Healthcare Directives: Ensure your medical preferences are followed.

Beneficiary Designations: Directly influence the distribution of specific assets, often outside of the probate process.

Buy/Sell Agreements: Allows your family to retain the rights to your business (and its profits) after you pass away, and often includes a source of funding to do so.

Consider consulting with an estate planning attorney like Destiny to understand the nuances of the process and ensure your plan complies with your state law.

Here are some common questions you can have your attorney address:

Who will inherit my assets?

Who will manage my affairs if I'm incapacitated?

How can I minimize taxes and avoid probate?

Are my beneficiary designations up-to-date?

You should also work with a financial advisor who specializes in business like Sarah to understand how to properly structure the financial end of your estate plan.

Here are some common questions you should ask your financial advisor:

How will my dependents be financially cared for if something happens to me?

How much life insurance do I need to protect my family?

Does my business also have a need for key person life insurance?

In the event I pass unexpectedly before reaching retirement or financial freedom, how will my family, employees and clients be protected?

Proper estate planning is NOT just about creating documents; it's about ensuring your wishes are carried out and your loved ones are protected. It's about considering how something happening to *you* could impact your clients and employees. This is typically a complex and critical process. You can do some of this on your own – and it is better than nothing when getting started; however, as you grow, make sure you seek the right professionals to ensure all those loose ends are tightened up.

This chapter is about how to put the proper legal protection in place so you can invest with less risk. How to invest responsibly. How to make sure your family, your employees and even your clients will be protected as well as your own wealth. My *Legal Protection RoadMap* is the exact formula to help you do this.

Let me break down each of the fundamental pieces of my *Legal Protection RoadMap*:

1. BUSINESS LEGAL PROTECTION - DIFFERENT ENTITY TYPES & CONSIDERATIONS

Choosing the right entity is like building a fortress for your endeavor. It can also be the most important part in protecting the wealth you are getting ready to build.

As an attorney for small businesses for nearly a decade, one of the most common misconceptions I continue to hear is that "I don't need that LLC (or any other type of legal protection) until I am making real money like 6-figures and above." This is absolutely incorrect and can lead to devastation and bankruptcy. For instance, it is entirely possible that you could get sued for something that you sold or did prior to your LLC being formed and YOU would then be held personally liable even if you have set up that LLC after the incident. This is SO important to understand.

Let's break it down even further.

A true "legal" entity – LLC, Corporation or Partnership – will provide a fence around your personal property. If you were to ever get sued or even threatened to be sued, they could not pierce that fence and get to you personally unless you are operating the business with no considerations for its structure.

In other words, if you are commingling funds, treating the business as you would yourself and not more of a manager, and holding your business out to essentially be yourself and not another entity – these things can get you in trouble and no amount of money or good operating agreement or Bylaws for your business will keep you from being personally liable. However, if you set in place a true legal entity and treat it as a "separate" entity from yourself personally (like not commingling your bank accounts from personal and business), the law will provide the full personal protection so that ONLY your business assets could/would be at risk if a lawsuit occurs.

When people talk about "legal" entities, they typically throw the word "sole proprietor" into the mix. However, many people do not truly understand what this means legally. In fact, "sole proprietor" is NOT a legal entity, but merely the default business entity structure that your business takes on once you start making income from sources that are not a W-2. A sole proprietorship is simply an individual operating a business; it's the default structure with no legal distinction between the owner and the business.

A sole proprietorship provides ABSOLUTELY NO LEGAL PROTECTION. Avoid this structure at all costs – **unless** what you are doing is simply a very low-risk hobby that makes a mere hundred dollars a month (but if you are reading this book, you are into building wealth, not hobbies).

The legal entity structures that most business owners will encounter and should consider are the following:

2. Limited Liability Company (LLC):

Liability Protection: Shields owners' personal assets from business liabilities.

Flexibility: Offers various management structures and tax options.

Pass-Through Taxation: Allows profits to flow through to owners' personal tax returns.
Characteristics:

Liability Shield: Provides personal asset protection against business debts.

Tax Flexibility: Options for taxation as a disregarded entity, partnership, or corporation.

Simplified Formalities: Fewer administrative requirements compared to corporations.
Strengths:

Complexity in Some States: Some states impose additional compliance and fees.
Weaknesses:

3. Corporation:

Separate Legal Entity: Exists independently from its owners (shareholders).

Limited Liability: Owners' personal assets are protected from business liabilities.

Stock Issuance: Allows raising capital by selling shares of stock.
Features:

Strong Liability Protection: Owners are generally not personally liable for business debts.

Capital Raising: Ability to attract investors through the issuance of stock.

Perpetual Existence: Continuity of the business beyond changes in ownership.

Strengths:

Complex Formalities: Higher administrative and regulatory obligations.

Double Taxation: Subject to taxation at both corporate and individual levels.

Weaknesses:

4. Partnership:

Shared Ownership: Involves two or more individuals in business ownership.

Distributed Profits: Pass-through taxation where profits are reported on partners' personal tax returns.

Shared Management: Partners share decision-making and responsibilities.

Attributes:

Shared Expertise: Pooling resources and expertise among partners.

Tax Benefits: Pass-through taxation avoids double taxation.

Flexible Structure: Various partnership types offer different liability protections.

Strengths:

Unlimited Liability: General partners are personally liable for partnership debts.

Disagreements: Potential for disputes among partners if roles and responsibilities are not clearly defined.

Weaknesses:

Each entity type has its own armor against liability; understanding these shields is critical for safeguarding personal assets.

If you don't know which one is best for your business, I encourage you to seek a professional to assess your specific situation – ESPECIALLY if you will be using it for protection in investment property. There are all sorts of additional considerations for investment property in setting up the legal entity – take it from me – someone who is analyzing this weekly, if not more, for clients (real estate investment is HOT!).

CONTRACTS & AGREEMENTS - THEY DO MORE THAN YOU KNOW!

I am sure you have all heard, have a written contract in place so that you get paid. OR – have that written contract in place so that everyone is on the same page and clear about what they are getting themselves into.

And, yes, these things are ALL important.

We want you to get paid and have the ability to enforce it properly in court if necessary; however, contracts can provide SO MUCH MORE THAN THAT in limiting your liability and protecting your wealth.

I truly believe that contracts are the unsung heroes of business dealings, defining the rules of engagement and safeguarding interests.

Picture this: a well-structured contract isn't just about putting pen to paper; it's another legal fortress shielding your business.

Let's talk about the key aspects of a contract.

In the world of contracts, specificity is paramount. Clear, well-defined terms minimize ambiguity and set expectations in stone. They become the backbone of trust, ensuring the parties involved understand their roles and responsibilities. But contracts are more than mere guidelines; they're protection mechanisms. They serve as legal tools to enforce obligations and protect your interests.

For instance, employment contracts meticulously outline terms of employment, including duties, compensation, and confidentiality agreements. Service agreements between businesses and clients or vendors lay down terms for services rendered, preventing misunderstandings.

Now, here's where it gets intriguing. Contracts can play a pivotal role in limiting a business owners' liability.

Let's consider this scenario: suppose you're an Uber driver. If an accident occurs while you're on duty, and there's a contract explicitly stating that Uber indemnifies the drivers for such incidents, that contract acts as your safety net. It shields you from personal liability, per the terms outlined in the agreement. This type of language is written in the agreement as a "Limit of Liability" provision or an "Indemnification" provision.

These types of provisions that limit a business owner's risk are the reasons why ChatGPT or any other Large Language Model (LLM) will not replace lawyers. They just don't know where and when these types of provisions are important because they can be so fact specific on your deal, business or arrangement and even state law. This is also why if you are looking to put a contract in place for a deal that is quite a bit of money or a contract you will be using day-in, day-out, I truly urge you to have an attorney at least look over the agreement you intend to use and make revisions so that you are protected to the max. Contract templates are a truly great place to start – and especially for small, start up businesses on limited resources – but don't make them a crutch.

Legal protection in your business is truly an INVESTMENT – not just an expense.

INSURANCE: PERSONAL & BUSINESS, A DUAL LAYER OF PROTECTION

Now that we have that fence in place, you should be asking yourself – well, if I got sued and my business was responsible, how do I pay that judgment or settlement?

Well, that is what insurance is for. We transfer that risk (or liability as discussed above) onto the insurance company to pay out that judgment or settlement so that your business does NOT go bankrupt.

When discussing insurance, it's vital we weave both the personal and business coverage into your protective tapestry–similar to prepping your personal estate plan above.

Let's start with the common types of personal insurance I hope you already have:

Health Insurance: A cornerstone of personal coverage, it shields against exorbitant medical expenses due to illnesses or accidents.

Life Insurance: Safeguards your family's financial future by providing a lump sum or periodic payment upon your demise.

Disability Insurance: Offers income protection if you're unable to work due to injury or illness.

If you have not already considered these, you want to. These personal policies, along with the umbrella policy discussed below, can form an even stronger fortress for your business castle. In fact, personal insurance often intertwines with business insurance, especially for entrepreneurs and small business owners. Also, some personal policies might provide supplementary coverage for certain business-related risks (as discussed below).

Personal insurance ensures your loved ones are financially protected in unforeseen circumstances. It also provides a safety net, allowing you to focus on business endeavors without constant worry about personal liabilities.

But, the question we get most when working with small businesses is:

What business insurance should I consider? What amount of coverage do I need (how much money would it pay out on a claim)?

We are going to give you a few considerations so you can "talk the talk" so to speak with your insurance agent, but, just know, that insurance coverage can be based upon so many factors including your locality and what types of products/services you offer so it is important at the end of the day to talk to a professional in the insurance industry about your specific needs.

However, here are some common policies that you can consider as a business owner:

1. General Liability Insurance:

Coverage: Protects against third-party claims for bodily injury, property damage, and legal costs.

Importance: Essential for safeguarding against common accidents and lawsuits.

2. Professional Liability (Errors & Omissions) Insurance:

Coverage: Shields against claims of professional errors, negligence, or failure to perform services.

Importance: Crucial for service-based businesses and professionals facing liability risks.

3. Property Insurance:

Coverage: Covers physical assets (buildings, equipment, inventory) against damage or loss due to specified perils.

Importance: Vital for businesses with physical assets prone to risks like fire, theft, or natural disasters.

4. Commercial Auto Insurance:

Coverage: Protects business vehicles used for work purposes against accidents, damages, or theft.

Importance: Essential for businesses with company-owned vehicles or employee-driven cars for business use.

5. Umbrella Insurance: A Game-Changer!

Definition: Umbrella insurance serves as additional liability coverage, extending beyond the limits of primary policies.

Extended Protection: Offers added liability coverage beyond the limits of primary policies.

Cost-Effective Solution: Provides significant coverage at a relatively low cost.

Dual Coverage: Can cover both personal and business liabilities under a single policy.

Benefits:

Versatility: Offers broader protection, bridging gaps and providing additional security against unforeseen liabilities.

When deciding on coverage amounts (how much your insurance will pay out for a claim), you really need to ask yourself – *will this amount be enough if someone sues me?*

To give you some perspective, in my days as a trial attorney, average settlements for small businesses in a slip-and-fall case typically ranged from a few thousand dollars to tens of thousands–even millions in some cases–depending on the severity of injuries, medical expenses, lost wages, pain and suffering, and other damages.

If this gives you any idea, lawsuits, being sued, or even threatened to be sued can get real expensive with attorney fees, costs, and medical bills from the injured client. You want to make sure you have a decent amount of coverage, because if you don't, they will then be looking to your business to pay out the remaining amount (or you personally if you don't have that proper legal structure in place as discussed above).

So...choose wisely.

REGULATORY & COMPLIANCE - I'LL KEEP THIS SHORT, BUT YOU CAN'T IGNORE IT

Ah, the complex labyrinth of rules and regulations governing industries. Here's what every savvy business owner needs to comprehend: Regulatory compliance isn't merely a box to tick; it's an essential part that will guide your business in the right direction.

Different industries dance to different regulatory tunes. Compliance isn't just a choice; it's a mandatory dance step to avoid penalties and legal entanglements. Each sector boasts its unique set of regulatory requirements, making compliance an absolute necessity.

Embracing compliance isn't solely about adhering to rules; it's about safeguarding your business. By meeting legal obligations and industry standards, you're erecting a protective shield around your operations. Compliance isn't just a safeguard against penalties; it's a testament to your commitment to legality and ethical operations.

Consider this: Complying with regulations isn't just a regulatory chore; it's a strategic move that limits potential liabilities, ensuring that your business sails through turbulent legal waters unscathed.

So, before moving forward in your business, at least research what your state, city, and county regulations are for your industry. These can vary greatly and are too often ignored and cost business owners hundreds and thousands in future fees.

INTELLECTUAL PROPERTY (IP) - SAFEGUARDING YOUR ASSETS

It is SO important to ensure that you are establishing a strong IP foundation and protecting it against other usage. This is especially important in America, as you can actually lose your IP rights if you don't – what the law calls - police them (or enforce your IP rights against someone who is infringing or stealing them).

IP encompasses trademarks, copyrights, patents, and trade secrets (and technically, design rights), serving as the bedrock of your uniqueness in the market.

So what are these?

Trademarks:

At its core, a trademark is the face of your brand, representing your business to the world. It encompasses symbols, names, logos, or phrases that distinguish your products or services. Trademarks serve as badges of authenticity and quality, fostering consumer trust and brand recognition. Think of iconic logos like the Nike swoosh or the golden arches of McDonald's – they're trademark powerhouses.

In the United States (not the case in other countries), trademark rights are predominantly established through usage rather than registration. The entity that first uses a specific mark in commerce for particular goods or services typically gains priority rights to that mark within the scope of its usage. This usage date becomes crucial in determining priority rights in cases of potential conflicts between two parties claiming similar trademarks.

Copyrights:

Ever marveled at a piece of literature, art, music, or software and wondered about its protection? Enter copyrights – guardians of creative expression. They safeguard original works of authorship, providing creators exclusive rights to reproduce, distribute, and display their creations. From novels and movies to software codes and architectural designs, copyrights shield a vast array of creative endeavors.

Patents:

Patents are the linchpin of innovation protection. They safeguard novel inventions, granting inventors exclusive rights to their creations. Whether it's a groundbreaking technology, a unique manufacturing process, or a new drug formulation, patents protect the fruits of inventive labor. Timing is critical in the patent world; timely filing is imperative to secure patent rights.

Trade Secrets:

Think of trade secrets as the mysterious hidden gems of IP. They safeguard valuable business information, from formulas and processes to customer lists and marketing strategies. Unlike other forms of IP, trade secrets thrive on confidentiality. They offer perpetual protection as long as they remain confidential and aren't publicly disclosed. These are typically made through Confidentiality - Non-disclosure agreements more than filing with the government or any public entity.

Design Rights:

Design rights guard the visual appearance of a product or its ornamental features. They protect the aesthetics that make a product appealing. Whether it's the sleek design of a smartphone or the unique shape of a bottle, design rights ensure exclusivity in appearance.

So now that you know what IP is, what are the steps you should be taking with it?

Ensure your creation does not infringe (steal, use) any other's already established IP

Properly protect your IP, including federally registering your Patent(s), Trademarks, & Copyrights (and having the proper NDA's in place for Trade Secrets).

Understanding the significance of IP is pivotal. It's not just about the logo or the product design; it's about safeguarding what sets your business apart from competitors. Your brand name, innovative products, creative content – these are the cornerstones of your identity and success. Protecting them is safeguarding your market position and preserving your competitive edge.

Note: Ensure You're Not Even "Accidentally" Using Someone Else's Intellectual Property

When starting a business, it's essential to check that your chosen name, logo, and other intellectual property does not accidentally infringe on (steal or illegally use) others' rights. I've seen cases where a seemingly small difference, like using numbers instead of words, could still mean infringement. A lot of my businesses are just simply naive to how trademark rights and infringement works. Or they just simply lack the knowledge to do the basic initial searches to ensure they can even use it.

For instance, my client had a business name (for the sake of this book) called "I work 4 you law," but there was already another business named, "I work four you law" with a spelled-out number four. Even though a search might not directly point to the same name, it could still be considered infringement if it's substantially similar, in the same area, and field (i.e. legal).

Infringement isn't just about directly copying; it also includes using substantially similar marks in the same field. So, it's crucial to conduct checks to avoid legal trouble.

The best option for conducting this search is to hire an attorney to do a full or what we call "comprehensive" search. A paid full or comprehensive search utilizes a third party to review and pull all sorts of public (and some non-public as not all state databases are public) information. The attorney then analyzes all sources pulled and provides you an opinion on any "troubling" marks (those similar or substantially similar in same or similar fields). This type of search runs anywhere from $600-750 per each mark or material at the time of this writing.

I am well aware that this cost can be outside the new business budget, so if you aren't quite ready for a full attorney search, at bare minimum, you should be completing these next steps every time you create a new Trademark or Copyright.

Here are steps for an informal search:

Google Search: Look up all variations of your business name. Run your logo and any slogans through it for same and similar variances.

Social Media Check: Explore EVERY social media platform including, Facebook, Instagram, Twitter, Snapchat, (even) Thread and others for similar names, trademarks, logos. Note that even a social media handle can be a Trademark.

USPTO Website: This is similar to Google and is for trademarks. Use the search engine at the United States Patent and Trademark Office (www.uspto.gov) to find any same or similar registered trademarks. You can also run logos, but this can get a bit tricky.

Additional Searches: Check any other relevant databases or platforms indicating trademark usage or similarities.

Although a thorough professional search is best, these steps can provide a starting point to spot potential conflicts or similarities in existing intellectual property. The last thing you want is to receive a cease & desist letter from another business ordering you to stop using their name, logo, etc., simply because you didn't check to see if it's in current usage by someone else.

As for patents, as discussed above, you will want to work with a patent lawyer on your invention. Having a lawyer will ensure your invention is not infringing upon someone else's patent. This should not be done on your own.

Federally Registering Your Patent(s), Trademark(s) or Copyright(s)

Once you've got clearance on the trademark or copyright (or patent through your patent attorney), this is where you will want to consider if federally registering that IP is necessary.

In the United States, securing your IP typically involves navigating the federal registration process. For trademarks, federal registration with the United States Patent and Trademark Office ("USPTO") offers heightened protection, granting exclusive national rights and legal remedies against unauthorized use.

Similarly, copyright registration with the U.S. Copyright Office ensures stronger legal footing and provides statutory damages and attorney's fees in case of infringement disputes. Remember, the copyright notice (©), while not mandatory, adds a layer of protection to your creative works. You can also do what's called a DMCA takedown which will actually take down the infringer website, social media channel, or the like just by sending in your copyright registration to the owner of the site/social media channel. It is such a cool tool.

When it comes to patents, timing is critical. Filing for a patent within the stipulated time frame after invention disclosure is crucial. The clock starts ticking upon public disclosure, and missing deadlines can lead to the loss of patent rights. You also must file that patent with the USPTO, somewhat similar – but much more involved application - as a Trademark. This MUST be done with a specifically licensed patent attorney.

While federal registrations offer robust protection, their absence (at least as to Trademarks and Copyrights) doesn't mean your IP is defenseless. Common law rights do exist even without federal registration, but they severely lack the same level of legal reinforcement and remedies and, as discussed in other areas, federal registrations *increase* the value of your business, your ability to use it as collateral on a loan, and can make a MASSIVE difference on the ultimate valuation of your business when you go to sell it.

Without a federal registration (at least on trademarks), you could also be severely limited in what geographic areas you use your name, logo, etc. For instance, let's say you have a coaching business and your clients are in Kansas and Missouri. You have not federally registered *any* of your Trademarks (name, logo, slogan, etc.). Yet, someone starts using your name and logo in Florida. Unfortunately, you will likely have no rights to stop this infringer from using your name/logo in Florida unless it was Federally Registered. In fact, you may have even lost your own later rights to then go into Florida and start marketing and gaining clients under that same name/logo!

This gets really tricky and is why when you're considering if you should federally register your IP, I always strongly encourage it if your business will be AT ALL focused on the brand you have created.

We won't get into it in this book (cause it could be another whole book in itself), but you should be generally familiar with enforcement strategies for protecting your intellectual property. There are a range of options including, employing cease-and-desist letters to halt unauthorized usage, pursuing litigation against infringing parties, or resorting to alternative dispute resolution methods like mediation or arbitration.

Safeguarding your IP isn't just a one-time task though; it's an ongoing commitment. Regular monitoring, surveillance, and proactive measures are essential and required. Implementing confidentiality agreements, non-disclosure agreements (NDAs), and trade secret protections within your business operations may be necessary. Not keeping an eye on your intellectual property and not taking action when someone uses it without your permission could lead to losing your rights over time. This is what we call "waiving" your rights in the legal system. It's like saying it's okay for others to use what's yours if you don't speak up and ask them to stop. So, staying proactive and taking steps to protect your IP is super important to keep it yours.

In essence, protecting your IP isn't just a legal obligation; it's a strategic investment safeguarding your business's identity, innovation, and competitive advantage.

So, there you have it. The five different types of legal protection you need to consider before you start investing, so you can minimize the risk to your family and build wealth with confidence!

***

Let's Reflect On This:

If something happened to you tomorrow, do you have confidence that your family would be okay financially?

All investing involves risk. Are you financially prepared to invest, without risking your family's future?

Let's check the boxes:

I earn more than I need for basic expenses. I can pay all my bills and have extra cash left over at the end of the month.

I have a Disaster Preparedness Plan, have identified the most likely scenarios, and have a fully-funded Emergency Fund to fall back on

I have life insurance to protect my family, employees and clients in the event that anything were to happen to me

I have an Estate Plan and Business Exit Strategy my family or employees could use in the event of my sudden demise to ensure the business survives the 60 day wait for insurance payout or up to two years of debate in probate court

My debts are all income-producing with a greater return than the interest is costing me, or I am debt-free

I have set up the appropriate business entity for the type of investing I intend to do (as advised by my attorney) and have a high business credit score so I can easily find funding if I need to

I have consulted an insurance agent and protected myself and my assets from losses too big for my Emergency Fund

I have consulted with an attorney and protected myself and my assets from potential lawsuits

How many "yeses" do you have? We have programs and courses that can address any "no's" on your list. When you're ready to tackle them, contact our team for support or a referral at:

For Finance & Insurance:

Sarah Nicole Nadler

www.FierceFeminineFinance.com

For Legal & Business Consulting:

Destiny Bounds

www.BoundforDestiny.com

   or

www.BoundsBusinessLaw.com

Chapter 8: Asset Alchemy

*S*arah

By now, you have identified your magic, written your A–Z statement to describe who it helps and how it transforms them, given it a name, and taken the proper steps to protect it legally. In other words, you don't just have an idea—you have an asset. Now comes the alchemy: turning that asset into passive income streams that pay you again and again.

This chapter is about leverage: how to find the right partners, collaborators, or systems that will pay you for the privilege of carrying your magic forward. Because wealth doesn't grow when you're the only one holding the work—it grows when you make your magic transferable, scalable, and licensable.

As I previously stated, the key to Asset Alchemy is the question:

Who has what I need,

And needs what I have?

Because if you can answer it, you can unlock partnerships where someone *pays you* for the privilege of taking work off your plate.

Finding The Right People To Partner With

My favorite way to do this is to license out your idea to other businesses or partners who will manufacture, produce or sell it for you (usually in exchange for equity or royalties).

Many women fail to earn passive income with their intellectual property because they lack the skill of negotiation so even when an opportunity falls right into their lap...they fumble it.

Like the time in 2020 when a Functional Medicine practitioner approached me about coming on as an expert inside his online coaching program for other practitioners.

I was new to the coaching/consulting world, and so excited by the fact that someone was impressed enough by my online content to want to pay me $1k/month to show up for his audience..that I jumped before I thought.

In addition to one coaching call per month, I also agreed to record an online course with my juiciest content for their members. In other words, I *gave away full rights to my intellectual property.*

The owner launched his coaching program and the sales started out strong but slowed down a few months in. Over time it became clear he and his business partner were struggling to bring in enough clients to make ends meet. I offered to help with marketing, but ultimately, he and his partner felt uncomfortable accepting my help for free, and they couldn't afford to pay.

I ended up leaving, but *my recordings stayed behind.* Due to the nature of the contract I signed, I had given up all rights to the content when I left the program.

I later realized how foolish it was to sign that contract. My income was entirely tied to trading time for money: if I didn't coach their clients, I didn't get paid. And even my intellectual property (the courses and training videos she recorded) were given over with no thought of licensing fees or royalties for their use.

This happens more often than you might think. Most authors who land deals with publishing companies sign their rights away, in whole or in part.

Even Taylor Swift fell prey to this, and made headlines when her music label refused to sell the rights to her music back to her! She had to leave the country and re-record all her songs...a move that was brilliant on her part, but how many singers could have pulled it off?

By the way, remember when we said that first you have to buy or build intellectual property that has true value? If you want a role model for this wealth strategy, follow Taylor Swift. She's a brilliant business woman who knows how to find a demand (women angry about their exes), popularize a product that fills the need (catchy songs). This is a perfect example of *The Passive Income Pathway Formula* at work.

Taylor could stop singing today and never go hungry as the brand deals she has signed and the music rights she now owns would continue to pay her every month for eternity. Like us, she is passionate about what she does and will probably continue to sing for many years...but she's also an example of what can go wrong:

To earn passive income, you need to find people to partner with who have what you need and need what you have, and put the proper protections in place so your partners don't become your future liabilities

Notice we didn't say: find partners you can trust.

A lot of investors have failed and lost their shirts because they tried to work with "trustworthy" partners. When the relationship soured, those very same people left them high and dry.

Most rational and good-hearted people will do the right thing if given a choice. It is when life throws us a curveball and makes a good person *feel* like they have no choice that you see decent people turn criminal.

Also, remember that story Destiny told you about? The one regarding her past business client whose so-called "friend" and partner just up and took everything in their spa business without notice and left her ...so she was forced to shut down and file bankruptcy.

The client clearly trusted her friend in the beginning. She trusted that this other person would not turn malicious and go back on their verbal word (or at least be fair).

Unfortunately, this is not the first time that either of us has had clients (and even lifelong friends) go into business over a handshake and a smile...only for circumstances to change and force one or both to make hard choices that hurt the other (and soured their relationship for life). Trust when we say, those past clients will never have a relationship with the partner that left and took everything.

It's not that we believe people can't be trusted. We both have many warm friends and close family!

But poverty, drugs, war, and threats to life or liberty make sane and good-hearted people do crazy things.

So rather than hesitating to get started because you don't know who to trust, or being *too* trusting and going into an investment with a handshake and a smile, let's look at ways to protect yourself: a) qualify the people you partner with, and b) put proper protection in place in case you're wrong.

QUALIFICATIONS

1. Someone who has what you need and needs what you have

If you have a proven method for teaching plumbers better customer service skills...*who has what you need and needs what you have?*

You could earn passive income by packaging up your magic into an online course and licensing it to:

Trade Associations

Plumbing Schools and Training Centers

Business Consultants

Plumbing Podcasters

Plumbing Business Networking Groups

Plumbing Service Review Websites

Plumbing Business Publications

Plumbing Certification Programs

Any one of these organizations or professionals might add your course to their platform, paying you royalties every month.

If you're a successful artist with a popular line of paintings (think= Thomas Kincaide) *who has what you need and needs what you have?*

Interior Designers

Art Galleries

Real Estate Agents (for staging homes)

Luxury Home Builders

Home Decor Brands (for reprints)

Chains of High-End Hotels and Resorts

Print-on-Demand eCommerce Stores

Every one of these types of people needs high-end artwork, and has a continuous stream of your dreamy clients to sell it to! By selling the rights to your work, you could live off the royalties for the rest of your life.

By identifying who has what you need and needs what you have, you will have a list of potential partners to turn your intellectual property into a fully passive income stream.

2. Noncompetitive

The ideal partner is one who serves the same audience as you but has no interest or ability to ever compete in your space.

When compiling your Top 100 List, it's important to only add partners who have a vested interest in your success. If one of the names or types of professional on your list has an interest in competing with you, delete them from the list.

This comes under the heading of *defensibility*. How defensible is your intellectual property? As Destiny detailed in earlier chapters, it is a good idea to have an attorney who specializes in patent, trademark and copyright law look over your list to identify potential weaknesses in your legal protection of your idea.

But, even a highly indefensible idea (one anybody could copycat) is relatively safe from a partner who has zero interest in competing with you and is vested in your success (i.e., one who has what you need and needs what you have).

The way you find such people is by networking. Build relationships deep enough that you can discover what the other person values most. And then make sure the contract you sign with them is fulfilling a deep-seated need or desire on their part.

3. Similar Values

The more we study the mind and what makes people "tick," the better deals we are able to close and the more confident we feel about the people we work with.

For me, even before I became an avid student of philosophy, I had a rule of thumb when it came to doing business or investment deals that has never failed me:

Don't Do Deals With People Whose Values Don't Align With Your Own.

Your core values are a fundamental part of your decision-making process. They guide how you respond to situations and people. Your values determine, to a large degree, the way in which you go about achieving success.

If a person has fundamentally different values than you, it is likely there will be a large clash of personalities or choices somewhere down the road.

Even when you don't know what another person's core values are in so many words (we don't often walk around dropping these in normal conversation), their lifestyle, choices, and vibe usually make it fairly evident.

How do they talk about other people?

What do they consider to be "good" behavior? Bad?

It isn't a question of whose values are "right" or "wrong," but rather *alignment* of values and shared goals that matter.

In other words, the fact that someone is of a different background, religious affiliation, or has different political leanings than me is *utterly irrelevant to any deal I might make with them.*

But their core values: honesty, innovation, excellence, commitment to a drug-free lifestyle...those are very relevant.

I won't do business, invest, or partner with people whose values are starkly different from my own. Not because I think mine are better, but because the difference between my values and theirs *will* cause conflict. It's only a matter of time.

Creative Funding

Destiny

Sometimes the partner you need to create a passive income stream is an investor. Whether you have an invention that needs funding for a prototype, an online course that needs to be recorded and beta-tested, or any other scenario where proof of concept requires capital you don't have on hand, creative funding can sometimes be necessary.

But bringing investors into your business isn't just about securing funding; it's also crucial to ensure that the process complies with legal standards and protects you in case the investment goes awry or one party breaches the agreed-upon terms of the deal.

And, believe me, the process is NOT simple. Understanding the legalities surrounding investor qualifications, types, and regulatory requirements is fundamental to safeguarding your business's integrity. Because they are so complex, I consult weekly with start-ups on this. If you bring on investors without considering the proper legal implications, I have no doubt it will kill your passive income stream before it even begins.

This information is to give you some basic knowledge so that when you're ready to discuss investors, you can have an informed conversation with a business attorney.

Investor Types and Legal Considerations

Before welcoming investors, it is essential to recognize that there is a diverse category of types of investors. And, each one carries its own type of legal requirements. Here are the basics:

Bootstrapping: When starting a business, individuals often rely on their personal savings, resources, and contributions from close friends or family members to fund the initial stages. This approach is a form of self-funding, where the entrepreneur uses personal finances or seeks financial support from their immediate social circle instead of seeking external investors or loans.

Bootstrapping with friends and family can involve various arrangements, such as personal loans, direct investments, or contributions in the form of resources (like equipment or workspace) to help kickstart the business. While this approach can offer more flexibility and autonomy in the early stages, it's crucial to still maintain clear communication and transparency regarding expectations, terms of the arrangement, and potential risks involved when involving friends and family in your business venture.

Bootstrapping does provide independence and control but may limit the speed of growth due to financial constraints. Although this is probably the simplest type "legally" to do, there are still considerations and agreements to put in place.

Qualified Investors: Also known as accredited investors, these individuals or entities meet specific criteria set by the Securities and Exchange Commission (SEC) in the United States – see more about the SEC below. To qualify, an individual must have a high income or substantial net worth. Entities such as banks, investment firms, and certain trusts may also qualify. Qualified investors have access to investment opportunities that are not available to the general public and may enjoy exemptions from certain SEC regulations. This can make bringing on Qualified investors a good idea in most cases.

Angel Investors: Angel investors, often referred to as high-net-worth individuals or accredited investors, are seasoned entrepreneurs, business professionals, or successful individuals seeking investment opportunities in promising early-stage ventures. These individuals inject capital into startups, typically in exchange for convertible debt or equity stakes in the company.

Beyond financial resources, angel investors bring a wealth of experience, knowledge, and valuable mentorship to the table. Their involvement goes beyond the initial investment; they often take an active interest in the success of the business. Angel investors provide guidance, strategic advice, and mentorship to the entrepreneurs, leveraging their industry insights and networks to help navigate the complexities of starting and growing a business.

Their contributions extend to offering valuable connections within the industry, facilitating introductions to potential partners, suppliers, customers, or even additional investors. This access to networks and mentorship significantly enhances the prospects of the startup's success.

Angel investors typically seek startups with high growth potential and scalable business models. They are willing to take calculated risks on innovative and disruptive ideas, aiming for substantial returns on their investments. However, their involvement might also come with expectations for a higher potential for growth and a clear exit strategy.

For entrepreneurs seeking angel investment, it's essential to present a compelling business proposition, demonstrate market traction, showcase a strong team, and articulate a clear plan for growth and scalability. Building a relationship with an angel investor goes beyond securing funding; it's about finding a strategic partner who can provide invaluable guidance and support on the entrepreneurial journey.

Venture Capitalists (VCs): VCs are investor groups or firms that inject significant funds into businesses, focusing primarily on startups exhibiting high growth potential. In return for equity ownership, VCs offer substantial financial backing and strategic guidance, often influencing the direction of the company. Their involvement typically extends beyond mere funding, as they provide resources, mentorship, and industry connections to foster the business's expansion. However, their influence may result in greater control over crucial decisions within the company's operations.

Crowdfunding: This method involves raising funds from a large number of people, typically through online platforms like Kickstarter, Indiegogo, or GoFundMe. It allows entrepreneurs to raise capital from the public, often in exchange for perks or early access to products rather than equity. Crowdfunding success often depends on effective marketing and presenting a compelling campaign to attract backers. There are all sorts of limits though on the amount of capital that can be raised through crowdfunding as per regulations imposed by the Securities and Exchange Commission (SEC). Different forms of crowdfunding, such as rewards-based, donation-based, or equity-based, each adhere to specific guidelines, offering opportunities for entrepreneurs to secure funds without necessarily diluting ownership or control of their business. However, navigating these platforms and ensuring compliance with regulatory constraints are essential factors for success in crowdfunding endeavors.

So, why do we even care about the "type" of investor? Well, some types of investors bring a WHOLE LOT of additional legal requirements from the SEC. These legal requirements are so complex, that I don't even deal with them – I send them to an expert in SEC law.

Navigating SEC Regulations and Exemptions

The Securities and Exchange Commission (SEC) is the regulatory body overseeing investment activities within the United States, primarily focused on maintaining transparency and safeguarding investors' interests. Within the SEC's regulatory framework, various exemptions exist for certain types of investors, offering them specific privileges and opportunities that might not be available to the general public.

For instance, qualified investors often benefit from exemptions that allow them to participate in investment opportunities with fewer regulatory restrictions. However, even when exemptions apply, certain obligations might persist, such as filing a Form D to notify the SEC about the offering without undergoing the comprehensive registration process required for public offerings. This form of disclosure helps provide transparency to the SEC and potential investors while enabling exemptions for certain types of investments. This is NOT something you can do alone.

Beyond financial capacity, you should also consider evaluating the investors legal structure (ensuring they have an LLC or Corp), their true funding capabilities (do they actually have sources with the money), and industry expertise. One of the major benefits in bringing on an investor is utilizing them for their previous business acumen and strategy alignment (think of "Shark Tank": everybody wants an investor who will be a good mentor.)

Then, once you have chosen the type of investor, a very strong investor (or the like) agreement is required. You want to ensure that an attorney is drafting this agreement because of the high stakes surrounding it.

When bringing investors into your business, it is crucial you navigate the legal obligations and consider the implications for each type of investor. This foundational understanding serves as a starting point, but engaging a business attorney for in-depth discussions regarding investor qualifications is highly advisable as the SEC truly does NOT mess around.

Summary

Those are the only five qualifications we have for business or investment deals:

Someone who has what you need and needs what you have

Noncompetitive

Good vibes

Core values aligned

Legally qualified investors

Everything else will iron itself out in the negotiation stage.

***

Let's Reflect on This:

First, identify who has what you need and needs what you have. Our favorite tool for brainstorming this is ChatGPT.

Here is the prompt we recommend:

"I need a list of examples of professions that would be in a Top 100 List (from Russell Brunson's book Traffic Secrets) for a _____. What type of businesses, brands, influencers and professions would I target to use the OPA method of attracting clients?"

Fill in the blank with the type of intellectual property you have, or industry, profession, etc.

Next, make a list of your core values so you can identify red flags when you begin to reach out to your list.

And lastly, review the list of types of investors and choose which one you are searching for and what your must-haves are so you'll know when you find them.

Chapter 9: Negotiating The Deal

We are about to embark on one of the most important chapters in this entire book. Getting this right means you will have the funds and people you need to succeed in achieving financial freedom rapidly and easily.

Getting this wrong can destroy any chance you have of financial freedom, or even land you in prison!

We are talking, of course, about the skill of negotiation. Doing it ethically, doing it effectively, and doing it profitably.

Earlier, we defined Abundance Mindset as:

1) the soul-deep belief that financial success is not a privilege: it is a duty,

and 2) an equally heartfelt certainty that your potential for success and wealth is limitless IF you apply the principle of *giving greater than expected value in exchange for money.*

Nowhere else will an abundance mindset be as important as when you enter into negotiations with a potential investor, partner, or when trying to license out your IP.

If you don't believe that your financial success is a duty;

If you're shaky on the value of what you bring to the negotiation table, or have the attitude that you're going to try to rip off the other party...

You will find yourself in hot water.

Negotiating requires finesse, strategy, and a keen understanding of the art of deal-making. Skills you will need to do this well are active listening, a cool head, and the ability to distance yourself emotionally from the outcome.

Preparing To Pitch

Sarah

For me, the most hair-raising part of any negotiation is the initial pitch. Whether I'm approaching the other party about a potential partnership, or making an offer to buy an investment, that first impression is crucial and I still get nervous beforehand every time.

It's important to note that not everyone is familiar with negotiation tactics, or feels comfortable counter-proposing. So pitching an offer that is at least in the right ballpark (of compensation or terms) is key to getting the conversation to *continue* long enough to find a win-win!

If you pitch too low, or don't understand what the other party values, you can unwittingly insult them, or come across as so amateurish or left-field that they won't take you seriously.

That's why preparation is vital before you pitch.

Even when someone else pitches an idea to me, if I see an opportunity to counter-propose something else, I take my time to prepare my pitch.

First, I research as thoroughly as I can without missing my window to close the deal. Understand current trends, asset values, and potential areas for growth. You have to know your numbers.

I start by ensuring I have a clear understanding of my budget, available financing options, and the potential return on investment. When discussing numbers during negotiations, confidence derived from a deep understanding of your own finances can give you a significant advantage.

Take a moment or two to clearly outline your own investment goals, risk tolerance, and criteria for a successful negotiation, without disclosing them to the other party. You will use them at the right moment during negotiations to close the deal.

Just as you've prepared your own list of musts and desires, do your best to anticipate what the other party might prioritize. Research them, their company if applicable, and ask questions early on to discover their goals, both current and long-term. This allows you to tailor your pitch and negotiation strategy to align with their interests. Not everyone defines success the same way! Making assumptions about what the other party needs and wants out of the deal can blow your negotiations before they ever get started.

Practice active listening. Get curious about the other party. I almost always lead with questions before I start in with a pitch. Discover what they value and what makes them "tick" before you open the negotiations. I have even started a conversation about partnering on an investment with the question: *"If I were to pitch you an idea I had on how we could _____ and earn passive income with it, what would you need such a partnership to do for you?"*

Armed with strong boundaries of your own, statistics and facts to drive your points home, an understanding of what the other party values, and a budget or financial projection of returns, you are ready to pitch your idea or offer.

Destiny

I began my career as a trial attorney, battling it out in high-stakes courtrooms, winning significant multi-million trials at a national top-notch law firm and conducting dozens of informal and formal meditations on cases.

Then, the pandemic hit, courts shut down, and suddenly, I found myself assisting friends diving into their own businesses, navigating the legal landscape – structuring, drafting contracts, and safeguarding their ideas. And guess what? I found a new passion in this small business world assisting entrepreneurs with their legal structure, contracts, and IP protection. No more trials for me.

Trial life taught me invaluable lessons about negotiation – I'd start with the advice – be direct, ask for what you want without beating around the bush. That straight-to-the-point approach was gold in the courtroom and mediations, and guess what? It's just as crucial in negotiations, especially for small business owners.

First, clarity and transparency are truly the name of the game. You must just communicate what you want, and do it plainly.

Also, being aware of common negotiation tactics – like anchoring – will help you steer discussions in your favor.

For instance, imagine you stroll into a flea market eyeing a vintage watch. The seller starts the game by quoting an initial price, say $500. Now, that $500 is the anchor – the starting point influencing your perception of the watch's value.

In negotiations, the first offer, or anchor, sets the tone and often serves as a reference point for subsequent discussions. Similarly, that initial price at the flea market influences your perception of the watch's value. From there, the negotiation dance begins – you might counter with a lower offer, say $300, aiming to meet somewhere in the middle for a mutually agreeable price.

Anchoring influences your judgment, just as the initial price at the flea market shapes your perspective on the watch's value. Understanding this tactic in negotiations helps small business owners navigate discussions more strategically, aiming for a favorable outcome while not getting tied down to the initial offer.

We used to use hard-core anchoring strategies ESPECIALLY at trial. If you heard counsel drop a million dollar number in their closing versus a thousand dollar number for medical damages, that substantially larger number could serve as an anchor to persuade a jury to give more. These are real things in the world of settling cases before trial as well.

(And I know Sarah stressed this earlier) But before stepping into any negotiation, preparation is truly everything! Just as I'd dive into research before a trial or even mediation, understanding market trends, valuations, and future projections is essential. Knowing your own financial landscape – goals, risk tolerance – gives you a massive advantage when numbers start flying.

Ultimately, my journey from a trial attorney to small business lawyer has taught me one thing – combining courtroom and mediation negotiation tactics with savvy strategies empowers small business owners to secure deals that fuel their success.

Whoever Controls The Conversation, Wins

Good manners dictate that you can't always be in total control of a conversation. Letting the other party guide where the talks go, and occasionally, interjecting with a curve ball is part of keeping a cool head.

But the InvestHER who cannot control a conversation; who lets the other party drawl on for thirty minutes or more about something off topic, or who can't work up the courage to interrupt a story with a friendly but on-point question, is likely not going to win many negotiations.

Negotiate means to reach an agreement by discussion with others. You don't reach an agreement by droning on and on about something else.

The first milestone in your negotiation is pinpointing the non-negotiables and preferences of the other party

Each succeeding milestone is a micro agreement in the direction of your own goal for the negotiation, as laid out before you began your pitch

The only way to achieve those micro agreements is to control the conversation, identifying barriers to agreement along the way, and offering win-win solutions to each barrier until you attain the end result of a signed contract.

Barriers to Agreement

The most obvious barriers to agreement in any negotiation are the terms and compensation plan.

Less obvious are the mental and emotional barriers, unspoken objections, red herrings, and negotiation "tactics" of the other party.

Negotiations are often full of stress, pressure, and uncertainty, which can trigger mental and emotional barriers. These barriers may manifest as fear of financial loss, a reluctance to trust, or concerns about the unknown that prevent the other party from wanting to continue the conversation or close the deal. The more you focus on acquiring the skill of Emotional Intelligence and practice Active Listening techniques, the better you will be at getting business partners, lenders and investors across the finish line.

***

Let's Reflect on This:

Do a self-assessment: Which of these negotiation skills do you feel confident about, and which need improvement:

Active Listening

Emotional Intelligence

Controlling The Flow of Conversation

Rebuttal and Counter-Proposing

Chapter 10: Using Legal As A Sword

D^{estiny}

Most people think of legal as a shield, and it is! Done properly, it will protect you from getting sued, being completely at fault, and stuck holding the bag (so to speak) when accidents happen.

But, when used properly, legal can also be a sword to *earn* you money (in your sleep in some cases).

We make the law work FOR US.

For instance, if you're a business that has a strong brand presence with trademarks you've properly registered and a patent on your inventions, when you go to sell your business or bring on investors, the fact that your intellectual property (IP) is legally protected can mean the difference between someone offering $15,000 versus $150,000! No joke!

So in this chapter, we'll explore ways that trademarks, copyrighted works, and patents can not only be leveraged to create passive income, but also increase the value of your business and the chances of your financial success.

Sarah

There are five paths to retirement that are only available to business owners. Asset Alchemy and monetizing your magic help every one of them. So let's go through them together:

Strategy #1: Sell Your Business To A Partner

As a successful $6+figure business owner, your company is probably one of the largest assets your household owns. And one of the ways you can use it in your retirement plan is to sell it once you are ready to move on.

In this chapter, we will discuss three ways to sell your business, but the first you should consider is to **bring on a partner** with the intention of having them buy you out of the business eventually.

This allows you to really ensure your clients will be served the way you treated them, as you will be training your replacement and documenting precisely how things are run as part of the transition.

Doing so provides two possible passive income strategies for you as the seller:

1) Your partner may take out a loan and buy you out with one lump sum. You can turn around and invest that lump sum into other assets that pay you passively, such as an annuity, real estate, etc.

2) Or you and your partner may choose to enter into a contractual agreement wherein the buy-out process extends years or even decades, which provides you with a potential for continuous income in retirement. This is called "owner financing."

When you prepare a partner buyout, documenting processes, frameworks, and client methods (Asset Alchemy) increases the value of your company. Instead of selling just a "book of clients," you're selling a replicable system—something far more attractive to buyers and easier for your successor to run.

You can structure the deal so your partner continues paying you royalties for use of your IP, even after you exit. That means you don't just walk away with a lump sum—you keep a passive stream for years.

Strategy #2: Find A Private Buyer

The second option is to **sell your business to a private buyer**. Look for a new graduate or up-and-coming professional in your industry, or an entrepreneur who wants to own their own business, without having to start from scratch.

Private buyers—especially new graduates or entrepreneurs—aren't just buying your business, they're buying confidence. If you've packaged your expertise into proprietary IP (methods, branded systems, digital products), it's easier for them to step in and succeed.

Think of it like selling a franchise. A company with protected IP assets is far more valuable and easier to finance than one dependent on your personal presence. Licensing agreements, trademarks, or digital products can even be carved out of the sale so you retain ownership of certain IP while still collecting royalties from the new owner.

Strategy #3: Obtain A Buyout Or Merger

Another strategy is selling your business to a corporation when you're ready to transition, so they can either take over or merge your business with theirs.

Selling to a corporation has numerous advantages.

It helps ensure you will get market value on your business at the time of sale, provides a cash injection into your household which you can use to fund a multitude of other investments, and leaves a legacy behind by ensuring your company will continue serving clients and the community.

Corporations value defensible assets. If your business has documented IP—courses, systems, brand marks, patents, or copyrighted content—it immediately increases your valuation. That's because corporations don't just want your clients; they want what differentiates you.

By packaging your IP as part of the deal, you create leverage. You can negotiate higher buyout terms or ongoing licensing agreements where the corporation pays to continue using your brand or methods. Protected IP shifts the deal from "client list acquisition" to "strategic asset acquisition," which usually commands a higher price.

Strategy #4: Build A Boring Business

Your fourth potential strategy for earning passive income as a business owner is to focus on building a boring business. As we covered early on in this book, this strategy gives you time freedom while still retaining full ownership of the business and access to its monthly profits.

The whole point of building a "boring business" is to step out of the day-to-day. But here's the truth: **boring businesses run on IP.** Documented SOPs, automated systems, training materials, and branded processes are intellectual property that make your business run without you.

When your team is trained on *your way* of doing things—codified into repeatable frameworks—you create scalability and stability. If your business is protected by trademarks or proprietary systems, you not only retain ownership but also make it far harder for competitors to copycat your model. That means you can stay hands-off and still collect steady profits with peace of mind.

Strategy #5: The BEST Way To Exit Your Business

The smartest retirement strategy isn't to put all your eggs in one basket. The safest path to financial freedom is to diversify—to combine your business exit with multiple streams of passive income.

That means mixing traditional investments (stocks, retirement accounts, annuities), tangible assets (rental properties, REI), and leveraged intellectual property income streams.

Here's why IP matters so much at this stage:

Sell the business, keep the magic. When your IP is properly documented and protected, you can sell your business *without* selling every part of your intellectual property. For example, you might sell your client list and operations but retain ownership of your digital courses, licensing deals, or trademarked method. That means even after the business has been bought out, some of your passive income streams continue to live on and become part of your investment portfolio.

Stronger safety net. Diversification protects you from risk. Real estate markets fluctuate. Stock markets can dip. But having royalties or licensing fees coming in from your IP adds another layer of stability. It's not about betting everything on IP—it's about weaving it into a broader portfolio of income streams so your retirement plan is resilient in any economy.

The truth is, most business owners dramatically overestimate the value of selling their business. Even highly successful practices or firms often sell for far less than expected. But when you combine that sale with investments *and* ongoing royalties from your protected IP, you don't just retire with a lump sum—you retire with a diversified, sustainable ecosystem of wealth.

That's why this is the best way to exit: it isn't just about selling. It's about building a portfolio of assets—financial, physical, and intellectual—that keeps paying you for decades to come.

Let's Reflect on This:

Look over the five ways your business can help you build wealth. Which appeals to you the most?

Based on the knowledge you have accumulated in this book, write out a five year plan of the Big Power Moves that you would have to take to make that goal a reality. What about your business needs to change? What professionals should you start building a relationship with to help you accomplish it?

For example, if you plan to sell your business and use owner financing to create a passive income stream, you should consider building a relationship with:

A business broker (to help you find a buyer)

An attorney like Destiny (to draft the contract and make sure you don't get cheated)

An accountant (to understand how the sale will impact your taxes that year)

A financial professional who specializes in business like Sarah (to help maximize the value of your business and identify where to invest the funds after you sell)

Chapter 11: Building Wealth on Your Terms

There are hundreds of ways a business woman can earn enough passive income to retire young and achieve financial freedom. Real estate investing, buying land, selling digital products, buying dividend-paying stocks...the list goes on.

Inside our *Confident InvestHER Academy* coaching program, we teach all of the above strategies, and more! But, as we mentioned in an earlier chapter, the method that stands out above the rest as being *uniquely perfect* for business women like us to begin with is using your intellectual property to earn licensing fees and royalties. It is rarely talked about and mostly misunderstood...and that is why we wrote this book for you.

Destiny

As an attorney and certified small business consultant, I see day-in and day-out how extremely intelligent business women can struggle to bring their visions to life. They think they have to do it all, be it all, and take on ALL the risks in their business.

Just recently...

I was sitting across from this brilliant lawyer – and very successful business owner at that! She was struggling with the notion that to make more money, she had to "work more hours." I know this is the case for SO many service providers, not just female attorneys. I simply said:

Have you thought about writing a book? Or making a course so you can make money in your sleep?

I gave her some examples of what you just heard about above regarding my story with Sarah.

It was like a light bulb just went off. Her entire face lit up. As she said:

Can I do that? How do I do that? Will you help me do this?

Of course, I said; I would help her and we have been working along each step, including:

Brainstorming and nailing down her passive income idea(s) using her own Intellectual Property;

Considering – who could she partner with on this idea? If anyone.

What legal contracts/agreements need to be written so that she maintains her intellectual property. (Remember, we don't want her completely selling her IP, only "leasing" it – in other words, "licensing". We want her to maintain the rights of her IP so she can use them elsewhere if she wants.)

Sitting back and enjoying the benefits of income in her sleep.

I know our businesses as females can truly become our "babies" -- I get this. But, at the end of the day, so long as we set our business up correctly, we are doing it in a way where it is a separate entity that we are running like a manager (see our above discussions on maintaining that limited liability protection; this is how we SHOULD be operating our business), we can truly learn to not exchange all our time for money, but be making that money in our sleep.

Sarah

As a multi-passionate entrepreneur, I often struggled with the advice I heard: to "niche down" and choose just ONE thing you're passionate about, as a way to earn a living.

My solution was to build a business, sell it, then build another one and sell that.

And it worked! I made plenty of money and was able to travel in between, living a very unique lifestyle; different from most women my age.

But it was exhausting. Bootstrapping a business with no outside funding is hard work. It means long hours and little financial security.

Once I uncovered *The Fear To Fierce Financial Formula*, I never looked back. Now, whenever I have a new wild crazy idea...

Like: "*Hey, why don't we move to Kansas and start a wedding venue, wellness retreat and organic farm!*"

...instead of trying to add it to my already busy plate, or fund it out of my own pocket, I follow the strategies we taught you in this book: create a separate entity to legally protect my existing assets, make sure I have enough Emergency Funds just in case, find outside funding to get started, network until I meet the perfect partners who have what I need and need what I have...

And voila! A new passive income stream.

Whether you're a solopreneur or have 20 employees, the proposition stands:

Why aren't we thinking like InvestHERs and using the resources that are ALREADY around us? Why do we limit ourselves (our potential, our thinking, our finances) to merely the things only we can do or who we can hire... and not turn our brilliant ideas into reality through licensing (selling) our ideas with the help of investment partners who already have what we need and are DYING for our new ideas?

As business women committed to shattering the confines of the hustle culture, we recognize that the ultimate power lies NOT in perpetually grinding but in leveraging our intellect. The true essence of success doesn't solely rely on burning the midnight oil. This is a fallacy we heard for too many years.

Success hinges instead on strategically planting seeds that yield perpetual harvests—the essence of passive income. And, as you know, at the height of this passive income pyramid sits our intellectual property.

Consider these unique ways that we have seen women use to leverage their intellectual property:

Personal Branding: Licensing a personal brand for self-help books, online courses, or branded merchandise. Collaborating with publishing houses for memoirs or inspirational content.

Unique Craft Patterns: Licensing intricate designs and patterns to craft stores for fabric, knitting, or crafting projects. Creating exclusive tutorials or DIY kits for crafting enthusiasts.

Beauty & Skincare Formulations: Licensing unique formulations to larger companies for beauty products or boutique spas. Offering specialized skincare routines through subscription services or online platforms.

Handmade Jewelry Designs: Licensing exclusive designs to manufacturers or retailers, expanding market reach. Crafting limited edition collections for specific events or seasons.

Workout Routines or Yoga Sequences: Licensing fitness routines to apps, gym chains, or online fitness platforms. Designing specialized sequences for yoga retreats or wellness centers.

Home Decor Concepts: Licensing themed room designs to interior decorators or home decor brands. Creating signature collections of home accessories for retail partnerships.

Children's Stories or Characters: Licensing characters for toy production or animated series development. Publishing children's books or interactive storytelling apps.

Sustainable Solutions: Licensing eco-friendly product designs to companies focusing on sustainability. Partnering with tech firms for innovative green solutions.

Digital Assets & Templates: Licensing website templates, social media kits, or digital branding assets. Designing customizable templates for content creators or small businesses.

Expertise-Based Licensing: Sharing specialized industry knowledge through online courses or masterclasses. Providing consultation services or speaking engagements based on expertise.

Innovative Tech Solutions: Licensing proprietary technological inventions to tech companies or startups. Developing software solutions for specific industry needs.

Culinary Creations: Licensing unique recipes or food concepts to restaurants or food brands. Creating signature product lines for grocery stores or meal kit services.

Educational Curriculum: Licensing teaching materials, curriculum, or e-learning modules to educational institutions. Developing specialized educational programs for niche markets.

Entertainment Concepts: Licensing scripts, show concepts, or performance rights to production companies. Collaborating on multimedia projects spanning films, series, or live events.

Health & Wellness Programs: Licensing wellness strategies, therapeutic methods, or holistic programs. Partnering with wellness retreats or spas for exclusive wellness packages.

Do any of these resonate with you? Spark new ideas? We know you have them! Embrace those ideas!

Embrace this new-found paradigm shift toward truly harnessing your intellectual property. We don't merely make financial choices; we redefine the very essence of our success through it. It's about planting seeds today that blossom into thriving orchards, yielding abundance tomorrow and beyond. It's about championing an environment where success isn't limited but contains an ever-expanding universe of possibilities. It is about leaving something to your family, your children, to your loved ones that will CONTINUE to make them money even when you are gone.

As we walk this path, let's remember: the key to unlocking financial liberation and reshaping success resides within us—within our ideas, within our creativity, within our intellectual property. It is ALL within us.

Let's embrace a mindset of abundance, reshape the narrative of our wealth, and step into a domain where passive income through our intellectual property transcends choice to become an everlasting legacy.

Sarah & Destiny

www.ingramcontent.com/pod-product-compliance
Lightning Source LLC
Chambersburg PA
CBHW071102290526
45795CB00004B/1616